the PERFECT GIFT

the PERFECT GIFT

UNWRAPPING **TRUE JOY** FOR CHRISTMAS

Barney Cargile III

Our Daily Bread
Publishing.

The Perfect Gift: Unwrapping True Joy for Christmas
© 2024 by Barney Cargile III

Scripture quotations, unless otherwise indicated, are taken from the Holy Bible, New International Version®, NIV®. Copyright © 1973, 1978, 1984, 2011 by Biblica, Inc.™ Used by permission of Zondervan. All rights reserved worldwide. www.zondervan.com.

Scripture quotations marked CEV are from the Contemporary English Version. Copyright © 1991, 1992, 1995 by American Bible Society. Used by permission.

Scripture quotations marked KJV are taken from the Authorized Version, or King James Version, of the Bible.

Scripture quotations marked MSG are taken from *The Message*, copyright © 1993, 2002, 2018 by Eugene H. Peterson. Used by permission of NavPress. All rights reserved. Represented by Tyndale House Publishers.

Scripture quotations marked NLT are taken from the *Holy Bible*, New Living Translation, copyright © 1996, 2004, 2015 by Tyndale House Foundation. Used by permission of Tyndale House Publishers, Carol Stream, Illinois 60188. All rights reserved.

In some cases, names and details have been changed to protect the privacy of the people whose stories are told.

Interior design by Michael J. Williams

ISBN: 978-1-64070-337-7

Library of Congress Cataloging-in-Publication Data Available

Printed in the United States of America
24 25 26 27 28 29 30 31 / 8 7 6 5 4 3 2 1

This book is dedicated to my wife, Linda. For fifty years she made Christmas a magical season for our family. Her childlike spirit and artistic creativity brought joy to our holidays in so many delightful ways. She is now with the angels worshiping the Savior whom she adored and whose birth she celebrated with such passion. She will forever remain my muse and source of inspiration.

Contents

Acknowledgments

I wish to thank my wife, Linda, who believed in me and always supported and encouraged me in my writing. Also, my grandchildren and great-grandchildren, who helped me see Christmas through the eyes of a child. In addition, thanks to my editor, Denise Loock, whose skills make my writing so much better. Finally, to the staff of Our Daily Bread Publishing, who took a chance with me and stood beside me during a difficult time.

Introduction

The season creeps in like a sluggish snail, then pounces like a hungry lion. We first notice it while walking through a department store. A familiar Christmas song wafts through the air (usually before Halloween) like auditory perfume. Then we find ourselves humming the tune. Without any effort on our part, Christmas spirit seizes our heart.

But that gentle heart-stirring nudge doesn't last long. Within a few weeks, we're battling traffic and fighting crowds in an effort to grab this year's Madison Avenue–driven fad our kids can't live without. Then we find ourselves in a tug-of-war to recapture that Christmas feeling, which abandoned us somewhere between the pajama aisle and the toy section.

For most of us, Christmas is the most wonderful time of the year. But if we're honest, we spend too many evenings collapsed in our recliner, exhausted from the holiday festivities. Besides shopping, there are parties, movies we've watched a hundred times, the hunt for the perfect tree, relatives (don't forget our precious kin), and the last-minute rush to grab a gift for the person who gave you something special but whom you overlooked when you were putting together your list. Before we can say "Ghost of Christmas Past," we discover we have much more in common with Ebenezer Scrooge than we do with jolly Saint Nick.

I'm not putting the kibosh on anyone's Christmas spirit. Quite the opposite. Like many of you, Christmas is my favorite time of year. This is what this devotional is all about. I present it to each reader as a Christmas gift—designed to bring joy to your holidays. I'm not so foolish as to believe it's going to brighten every moment when you're tempted to shout "Bah, humbug" at the top of your lungs in the middle of a store, but it may lift your mood a bit.

Beginning December 1, each day contains two devotions to carry you through Christmas Day, with a bonus meditation for December 26. They represent fifty-one ways to experience the story we love—the greatest story ever told. My prayer for you (and for myself) is that in the midst of our hectic holiday hassles, we'll discover a bit of joy as we remember the true meaning of Christmas.

The Messiah of Our Mess

Imagine you're stopped at a construction site, and a laborer passes in front of your vehicle. He's dressed in work clothes, covered in dirt and sweat. His face exhibits a day's growth of beard, and his hair is messy from toiling for hours. He's trudging to who-knows-where, hungry and exhausted from a hard day's work.

Nothing unusual. But what if somehow, in some way, you discover this carpenter is actually God. God come down in the form of a man, a working-class craftsman. It doesn't seem right. If God became a man, surely he would be decked out in a custom-made suit and luxury loafers or, even better, some heavenly attire we've never imagined. Certainly not a sweaty, dirty, exhausted carpenter. That wouldn't make sense.

But that's exactly what God chose to do. When God broke through into our world, he didn't just stick his toe in; he dove in headfirst. Hebrews 2:17 says that Jesus chose to be "fully human in every way." Why? Because God wants you to know that he knows how you feel. He became a mess, because our lives are messy. This is why we need a "Mess-iah." He's the Messiah of our mess.[1]

The nativity story is immersed in messiness. For starters, consider the Messiah's genealogy. In Matthew 1, four women are mentioned in his lineage—extremely rare in the ancient world. But even stranger, three of them were of disreputable character. Tamar conceived her child in an act of incest. Rahab was a prostitute, and Ruth was an idol-worshiping heathen. If I were writing the story, I'd try to keep these genealogical skeletons locked in the closet. But not

God. He shines a spotlight on them. Why? He wants us to see that Jesus meets us in the middle of our mess.

Then there's the mess of the Messiah's conception. Who in their right mind believed the crazy story that the Holy Spirit was Jesus's father? In first-century Israel, a cloud of questions would have hung over both Mary's and Joseph's reputations. These same questions followed Jesus for the rest of his life. It was a mess.

And what about the mess of the manger? Literally. Joseph probably had to push aside cow manure so Mary could lie on clean straw and give birth to the Son of God. This is no way for the Ancient of Days to be born.

When God chose to enter our world, he saturated himself in our mess. So we can relate to him. So we can value the sacrifice he made. And so we can know he understands what we're going through. That's Jesus . . . the Messiah of our mess!

Principle

God entered fully into our mess by becoming a man.

Ponder

- In what ways can you appreciate Jesus—the Messiah of our mess—in your life?
- Think of a time when Jesus met you in the middle of your mess. What was the outcome?

Pursue: For a deeper dive, study Matthew 1:1–17.

Jesus, I praise you for being the Messiah of our mess. Thank you for diving headfirst into every detail of our human experience.

Playing Santa

Have you ever taken pictures of a screaming kid sitting on Santa's lap? I suspect most parents have been guilty of this atrocity at least once. Linda and I certainly were culpable of this criminal behavior. Both our adult children are offenders as well. Children are usually fascinated with Saint Nick, but around age two or three, they enter the Santa-screaming stage—terrified of the jolly old man. A few years ago, my perspective of the whole photo-with-Santa tradition changed.

A local mall drafted me as a weekend substitute for Santa Claus. You can imagine what an intimidating experience it is to be a fill-in for the "real" Santa! On a scale of 1 to 10, my Santa meter ranked a solid 2.5. Not too impressive. As I sat on my simulated North Pole throne, dozens of kids lined up to share their Christmas wishes. A few items on their lists were downright heartbreaking—"Please bring Daddy back" or "Help Mommy stop drinking."

But it was the screamers who altered my perspective. The whole Santa concept is an oxymoron. We lecture children about the danger of talking to strangers, and what do we do? Plop them down on the lap of an old man wearing a red velvet suit. Then we refuse to rescue them as they scream for help. It seems a bit . . . I don't know . . . twisted, maybe?

If nothing else, this experience emphasizes the gigantic gulf between Jesus and Santa Claus. In Mark 10:13, we read of people bringing their children for Jesus to bless. The ever-clueless disciples rebuked the parents. Then Jesus rebuked the disciples. He called the little children to him and held them. I don't believe there were any screamers in the whole bunch. Why not? Because Jesus was the real deal.

I was a poor substitute for the "real" Saint Nick, and Santa Claus is a poor substitute for Jesus. What we long for more than anything else, Santa can't provide. I have nothing against Father Christmas, but he doesn't fill our deepest need for oneness with our Creator. Only Jesus can do this. Trying to find fulfillment in Santa, or anything else this world offers, will only lead to sorrow. Just ask the parade of two-year-olds crying on my lap.

Principle

Only Jesus can fill the deepest need of our heart.

Ponder

- How do you envision Jesus's interaction with little children?
- What do you long for deep inside that only Jesus can provide?

Pursue: For a deeper dive, study Mark 10:13–16.

Lord Jesus, thank you for the picture of you and the children. It stirs my heart to love you more.

It's Too Simple

In the 1950s, the Betty Crocker Corporation developed a cake mix with a basic formula. The box contained everything required to create a prize-winning cake. Simply add water. The product hit the shelves and . . . totally flopped. The corporate executives were bewildered. The simple mix should have produced instant success. They followed up with a market survey and discovered the problem: it was *too* simple. In those days, homemakers didn't trust a cake mix that only required adding water. So, the company pulled the product from the shelves and changed the formula, requiring the cook to also add an egg. Voila! Success.

Aren't we humans peculiar? We spurn the simple and create ways to complicate pretty much everything, including God. Think about it. What could be simpler? God entered our world as a baby and grew into a man. At the age of thirty, he set aside his tool belt and traveled the country with a simple message: God loves you. Then he died for us and rose from the dead. Simple, yet profound.

In Luke 18:17, Jesus said, "Anyone who will not receive the kingdom of God like a little child will never enter it." God doesn't ask us to perform near-impossible feats, like walking a mile barefooted on crushed glass, to experience salvation. Just receive his gift. Simply let him love you. How hard can this be?

For some, it's simply too, well, simple. Many stumble over God becoming man. Ridiculous. The Creator taking on our weaknesses? Absurd. The Almighty experiencing hunger, heartbreak, and humiliation? This makes no sense.

In Yann Martel's *Life of Pi*, a Hindu boy hears the story of Jesus for the first time. After describing Hindu gods coming to earth with "shine and power and might," he states, "This Son, on the other hand, who goes hungry, who suffers from thirst, who gets tired, who is sad, who is anxious, who is heckled and harassed . . . what kind of god is that? It's a god on too human a scale, that's what."[2]

Indeed. Who wants a God like that? I do. Maybe God's plan is too simple—too human—for most. But millions find comfort in the truth that he understands our struggles, that he's been where we've been. Simple? Oh yeah. But it's real, and it's true. Think about this the next time you take a bite of cake.

Principle

God's plan is too simple for many to grasp.

Ponder

- What aspect of God's plan to save us is most difficult for you to wrap your mind around?
- During this Christmas season, what can you meditate on to help you appreciate his simple plan more deeply?

Pursue: For a deeper dive, study Psalm 131.

Lord God, even before time began, you had a plan to save us. I praise you for your simple yet profound plan. Help me trust you, knowing I don't need to understand it all to believe it all.

Saved by a Baby

Debbie McIntosh should have been home on March 2, 2012, along with her daughter, Angela, and her son-in-law, Adam. As it turned out, had they been at their house in northern Kentucky, they'd all be dead. Instead, their lives were spared—by a baby boy.

Angela, who was five days late giving birth to her first child, went into labor early in the day. After rushing her to the hospital in Edgewood, Kentucky, the family anxiously awaited the arrival of their little bundle of joy. Then disaster struck. A tornado hit the town. In the midst of Angela's delivery, patients were moved to the hospital basement. As large hailstones struck the ground and tornado sirens pierced the air, she delivered a healthy boy. Aedan Douglas entered the world at 4:44 p.m. His mom, dad, and grandma welcomed him with loving arms.

The next day, Debbie returned to her property and found her former home reduced to a six-foot pile of rubble. Gathering the few items that remained, she sobbed over her family's devastating loss. Then she recalled the incredible joy of her grandson's new life. A stunning realization struck her. Little Aedan's birth had saved the entire family's lives.[3]

It's hard to contemplate such a scene, isn't it? Imagine delivering a baby boy in the midst of such chaos. Imagine a woman experiencing the anguish and struggles of childbirth while being denied the opportunity to deliver her firstborn, a son, in a suitable place. Imagine being forced to give birth to this child at a site totally inappropriate for such a critical moment. But what strikes me most is the realization that the McIntosh family were all saved by the birth of this baby boy. I'm sure we can't imagine such an event ever taking place. Or can we?

I recall the story of a baby whose birth saved not only the lives of one family, but also brought salvation for all humanity. In Luke 2:30–32, the prophet Simeon held baby Jesus and declared, "I have seen your salvation, which you have prepared for all people. He is a light to reveal God to the nations" (NLT).

God's blessings transcend every situation—no matter how heartbreaking, no matter how difficult—whether it's a baby who saves his family or a baby who saved the world.

Principle

Jesus was born to save all humanity.

Ponder

- Put yourself in Debbie's place. How would you feel, realizing that in the midst of devastating loss, your life was saved by the birth of your grandson?
- In the midst of loss, how can you allow Jesus to heal your heart?

Pursue: For a deeper dive, study Romans 8:26–30.

Lord Jesus, I welcome you into my heart once again during this Christmas season. Even in the midst of loss, fill me with a sense of gratitude for your arrival.

A Leprous God

In 1873, Father Damien landed on the Hawaiian island of Molokai in a boat carrying cattle and lepers. His destination was the village of Kalawao, a leper colony. He chose to make his home with them, and for the next sixteen years, shared his life with the lepers. He learned to speak Hawaiian. He treated their wounds through his touch. He embraced them, preached to them, and organized schools and choirs. Assisted by patients, he constructed houses and planted trees. He built two thousand coffins by hand so people could be buried with dignity. Slowly, Kalawao became a place to live, rather than a place to die, because Father Damien offered hope.

The people grew to love him. He wasn't just on their island; he was in their skin. He chose to live as they lived and eventually died as they died. After twelve years among them, he contracted leprosy, and died four years later, at age forty-nine.[4]

Imagine someone intentionally choosing to leave the comforts of home and coming to a place of disease, danger, and death. Imagine him taking on himself the people's affliction. Isn't this the story of Christmas?

We're all cursed with spiritual leprosy. This is why God entered our world. Born in the humblest circumstances, Jesus fully embraced our humanity. He lived as we live and died as we die. Philippians 2:6–8 states concerning Jesus, "Who, being in very nature God, did not consider equality with God something to be used to his own advantage; rather, he made himself nothing by taking the very nature of a servant, being made in human likeness. And being found in appearance as a man, he humbled himself by becoming obedient to death—even death on a cross!" The Son of God didn't merely dabble in humanity. He fully embraced our human condition, yet without sin.

This is why we celebrate his arrival on our planet. God came and embraced our leprosy. Much more than Damien could do, however, Jesus brought healing for our sinful condition. For this we worship him. Pause and reflect on when God arrived and took upon himself our spiritual leprosy.

Principle

Jesus not only embraced our spiritual leprosy; he healed us from this affliction.

Ponder

- What's your response when you realize all Jesus sacrificed to save you?
- How can you demonstrate your gratitude throughout this Christmas season?

Pursue: For a deeper dive, study Philippians 2:5–11.

Lord Jesus, no words can express how deeply grateful I am for the sacrifice you made for me by entering our world and dying for me. Throughout the Christmas season, remind me of this.

A Foolish Innkeeper

A young boy had his heart set on playing Joseph in a Christmas pageant, but a different lad landed the part. The disappointed boy settled for the role of innkeeper instead. Embittered, he determined to take revenge. On the night of the performance, Joseph knocked on the door of the inn and asked for a room. Rather than turning Joseph and Mary away, however, the innkeeper enthusiastically replied, "Sure, we have lots of room! Come on in!" But the boy who had earned the part of Joseph demonstrated his superior theatrical skills. He looked into the room and exclaimed, "What a mess! I can't let my wife stay in this dump. Let's go, Mary. I'd rather sleep in the barn than this place!"[5]

We laugh, but how many of us, like the bitter young thespian, would try to change the story? The Son of God lying in a manger. Really? He deserves a gilded, fleece-lined crib at the very least. And his parents? A peasant and his teenage fiancée—scratch that. The first worshipers? Not a bunch of shepherds. How about a contingency of religious leaders, kings, and maybe throw in some wise men? (Well, at least I got the last part right.)

One small problem. Except for the wise men, none of this was God's will. Clearly the plan was for Jesus to be born in the humblest of places, and the Almighty providentially arranged circumstances so there would be no room for them in the inn (Luke 2:7).

How often do we act as if we're smarter than God? We know what God's Word says, but, like the young innkeeper, we go off script and crash and burn. Think about Abraham and Sarah. Rather than trusting God to give them a child, they took matters into their own hands to help God out. The results were disastrous (Genesis 16).

God's way is always best for our lives, even when it doesn't make sense to us. This is true whether we're managing our finances, our family, or our future. If we surrender to God's plan, we'll experience results far better than we could imagine.

Let's not go off script like the foolish innkeeper. Trust God, even when his plan doesn't seem to make sense. Even if it means life may be hard for a season. God's plan is *always* better than ours . . . even though it meant the Messiah was born in a stable.

Principle

God's plan is always better than ours.

Ponder

- When have you learned the hard lesson that your way definitely doesn't work as well as God's?
- In what areas of your life are you struggling to surrender to the Lord?

Pursue: For a deeper dive, study Luke 2:1–7.

Lord, I willingly acknowledge your ways are far superior to mine. I surrender to your will. Help me trust you with my plans rather than be a foolish innkeeper.

The God of Surprises

I parked a few doors down, not wanting to spoil the surprise. My sister and I had concocted an unexpected treat for my father's seventy-fifth birthday. I made up some lame excuse for not attending his party, but it was a trick. On his birthday, I flew in and rented a car. Just before reaching Dad's house, I phoned him, expressing my heartfelt regrets.

Dad and I continued talking as I approached his home, then rapped on his door. He ignored my knocking. I pounded harder. Eventually he opened it, and we stood face-to-face, holding our phones to our ears. He froze, staring in confusion. Finally, reality hit him. I was standing there in the flesh. Overcome with emotion, he broke down. Truly a rare moment I'd like to freeze-frame.

I could have wished him a happy birthday over the phone and uttered the exact words I said in person, but it meant so much more for me to physically show up on his birthday. My presence was his present.

You think we love surprises? God is the greatest surprise artist of all. Nowhere is this more apparent than in the Christmas story. The angel Gabriel comes to Mary, announcing she—a virgin—is with child. Surprise! Joseph discovers she's pregnant. Surprise! An angel informs him Mary's telling the truth. Surprise! They travel to Bethlehem, and Mary's delivery room is a stable. Surprise! Shepherds drop in to worship their son. Surprise! The story also includes the surprises of Zechariah and Elizabeth, and of Anna, Simeon, and the Magi. Surprise, surprise, surprise!

Consider how amazing this is: The Creator of the universe desired to be physically present with us, so he dropped in for a surprise visit as a baby. Instead of merely leaving us a message, he showed up in person as the Living Word—the greatest present ever given. John 1:14 reveals, "The Word became flesh and made his dwelling among us." One of the names for Jesus is Immanuel, "God with us" (Matthew 1:23).

The God of surprises knows how to throw a great surprise party. If you get surprised this Christmas by a wonderful gift, just know God is smiling . . . because more than anyone else, he loves a good surprise.

Principle

God is the greatest surprise artist of all time.

Ponder

- Of all the surprises in the Christmas story, which is most meaningful to you?
- When has God surprised you with something wonderful?

Pursue: For a deeper dive, study Genesis 45:1–15.

Father, thank you for surprising me in wonderful ways. Throughout this season, help me grab hold of the surprises you have for me.

Prince of Peace

Christmas Eve, 1914, on the frozen Western Front in the early days of World War I. The Germans huddled in their bunkers; the Brits and French hunkered down in theirs. In between stood no-man's-land. Anyone who ventured from his trench would be shot by the enemy. In the frozen silence, a song rose from the German bunker. "*Stille Nacht. Heilige Nacht . . .*" As it died away, the British picked it up. "*Silent night, holy night . . .*" The Germans responded with "*Adeste Fideles,*" and the Brits echoed.

Eventually, a few Germans could no longer contain themselves. Leaving their trenches, they walked into no-man's-land as their officers attempted to restrain them. The British and French joined them, grasping one another's hands in warm greetings. For hours they sang together, exchanged small gifts, and shared food and family photos. For this brief time, they were no longer enemies, but fellow humans united by worship of the Christ Child.

Our faith in Jesus can unite us, even in the midst of war. Isaiah 9:6 prophesies Christ would be called "Prince of Peace." Ephesians 2:17 states that Jesus reconciled Jews and Gentiles by bringing "peace to you who were far away and peace to those who were near." No two cultural groups were ever more divided than first-century Jews and Gentiles. But Jesus made them one, as he continues to do today.

I'll never forget worshiping with a small church in the Arab Quarter of Old Jerusalem. Their pastor was a Palestinian Christian, and his associate was a Jewish believer. They had every reason to hate each other, yet they worked together, united by their love for Jesus.

As our leaders struggle to bring about peace on earth, God's Word tells us the answer is Jesus, the Prince of Peace. Not only in the Middle East, but worldwide. If this was true between Germans and Brits in World War I and Jews and Gentiles in the first century, if it's true between Arabs and Israelis today, how about in our own corner of the world? This Christmas, let's do more than go through the motions. Let's allow the Prince of Peace to reign in our hearts and transform our relationships.

Principle

As the Prince of Peace, Jesus unites enemies, even in the midst of war.

Ponder

- In what areas of your life are you neglecting to allow Jesus to reign as Prince of Peace?
- With whom do you need to pursue peace? How will you take the first step in establishing peace?

Pursue: For a deeper dive, study Ephesians 2:11–22.

Prince of Peace, fill my heart with your supernatural peace this Christmas and help it overflow to others, allowing them also to experience you as the Prince of Peace.

Light of the World

Even a birthday candle would have made a difference. We were visiting friends in the country, and I needed to grab something from our car. Because it was a dark, moonless night, our hosts offered to lend me a flashlight. I declined, then reconsidered when I stepped onto their porch. But my ego got the best of me, and I forged ahead. Attempting to navigate my way in the dark, I bumped into a stump in their yard and fell face-first onto the ground. Bruised and scratched, I grabbed the stuff I needed and headed back to the house, feeling like a prizefighter who'd been whipped by a ten-year-old.

During Christmastime, we're inundated with light. We climb onto our rooftops to run strings of glowing bulbs. We venture out on frigid nights and drive through neighborhoods to catch glimpses of the twinkling luminescence. Lights brighten our holiday season.

The Bible consistently uses light as a metaphor of righteousness and truth. In speaking of Jesus's advent, John 1:9 declares, "The one who is the true light, who gives light to everyone, was coming into the world" (NLT). Verse five observes, "The light shines in the darkness, and the darkness can never extinguish it."

Light is essential. Ever try to find a light switch in a pitch-black room? We stumble around, groping the walls, maybe even tripping and breaking things. The same is true spiritually. Without Christ's light, we stagger as we attempt to navigate our way through this dark world. This is why Jesus was born—to reveal the light—and to give us answers to the questions that plague us most. "Why am I alive? What's my purpose? What happens after I die?" Matthew 4:16 promises this concerning Jesus: "The people living in darkness have seen a great light; on those living in the land of the shadow of death a light has dawned."

Perhaps it's been a tough year. Maybe the darkness feels overwhelming. Don't despair. God sent His Son to bring light into our dark world. Breathe easy. Jesus offers hope. He truly is the Light of the World.

For me, this assurance is like a lifeline tossed to a drowning man. Christmas reminds us of how desperately we need the light of Jesus to fill our hearts. Let's lift our eyes above the darkness around us and open ourselves to the light of Christ. Then we won't trip on the stumps in our lives.

Principle

Jesus is the Light of the World.

Ponder

- What struggles have you experienced this past year?
- How does understanding Jesus as the Light of the World offer hope?

Pursue: For a deeper dive, study John 1:1–14.

Jesus, thank you for bringing light into our dark world.
Without your light, our world would be unbearable.

Keeping Christ in Christmas

We're often reminded to "Keep Christ in Christmas." However, an incident in Hamilton, New Jersey, gave the term a new twist. A baby Jesus figure was stolen from a nativity display in a residential neighborhood. The Christ-nappers left a ransom note demanding $800, informing the owners they better pay "if you ever wanna see your baby Jesus again." The doll had been purchased from Sears for a mere $69. A police spokesperson said the case "smacks of kids playing a prank." The ransom note was especially revealing, as it was signed, "Me, him, and the other kid who was really scared and didn't want to take your baby Jesus and the whole time was saying stuff like, 'You're going to hell.'"[6]

This time of year, nativity scenes are a significant part of our landscape. Each time I pass one, I'm blessed to remember the incredible gift of God entering the world as a baby. Yet as wonderful as the idea is, "Keeping Christ in Christmas" isn't what God has in mind. God desires that his followers enthrone Jesus as Lord in our hearts 365 days a year—not just as a yard ornament for a few weeks in December. First Peter 3:15 instructs us, "In your hearts revere Christ as Lord. Always be prepared to give an answer to everyone who asks you to give the reason for the hope that you have. But do this with gentleness and respect."

During the Christmas season, we probably have more opportunities to give the reason for our hope than at any other time. Folks' minds are centered on the incarnation. Manger scenes, one of a multitude of ways to proclaim our faith, dot our landscape like prairie dogs in North Dakota.

By all means, seize the moment. Share with others the hope you have in Christ. But remember the last phrase of Peter's instruction: "Do this with gentleness and respect." For too long, we've undermined our witness by coming across as judgmental and self-righteous.

Pray for opportunities, then open yourself up as a conduit of Christ's love and truth to others. Model his love to everyone you meet. Let another haggard shopper take that perfect parking spot at the mall. Smile and speak words of blessing to a weary clerk. Keep Christ in Christmas . . . and New Year's Day . . . and Groundhog Day and . . .

Principle

Keep Christ in Christmas every day of the year.

Ponder

- On a scale of one to ten, how well do you model the love of Jesus to others?
- How can you do this more effectively this holiday season?

Pursue: For a deeper dive, study 1 Peter 3:13–17.

Lord Jesus, forgive me for the times I don't represent you well. Fill me with your Holy Spirit so I can recognize opportunities to be a conduit of your love.

The Perfect Gift

Looking for the perfect Christmas gift? How about a trip to Portugal and handmade personalized dinnerware for $80,000? You can also buy a Roaring Twenties Party at the legendary Apollo Theater with your name in lights for $395,000. Or for a mere $235,000, you can receive ski lessons from international champion Lindsey Vonn. These are actual gifts found in the 2021 Neiman Marcus Christmas catalog.[7]

Okay, so maybe a Roaring Twenties Party isn't at the top of your Christmas list. But most of us, at some point during the holidays, feel the tug of materialism. It's a battle. Advertisers expend billions of dollars to entice us to spend, and so we spend more and buy more—whether we can afford it or not.

According to the National Retail Federation, on average, Americans spend nearly a trillion dollars on Christmas each year. But does getting more stuff increase our joy index?

Here's an idea. What if we asked our friends to donate money to a nonprofit organization or charity instead of giving us a gift destined for a thrift-store bin? Or what if we told extended family members we made a donation in their name to a charitable cause we believe in? Our church family did this, and we built fifteen wells in third-world nations for people who needed clean drinking water.

Even within our immediate family, we could cut back. Christmas after Christmas, my grandkids receive all sorts of expensive gifts, then spend the afternoon building a fort out of the cardboard boxes that contained the gifts.

Please don't misunderstand. God blesses us with material wealth and wants us to enjoy it. First Timothy 6:17 tells us that God "richly provides us with everything for our enjoyment." But he warns us that materialism can be a "temptation and a trap" that can "plunge people into ruin and destruction" (v. 9). We can get so caught up in gift-giving that we miss true wealth—spiritual and relational riches. In our pursuit for the perfect gift, it's easy to forget God's perfect gift to humanity.

Materialism is a continual struggle, but victory is critical. When we triumph, we'll discover riches far greater than $80,000 dinnerware—even if it includes a trip to Portugal.

Principle

Especially at Christmas, we need to battle the lure of materialism.

Ponder

- How can you get the most out of Christmas without getting caught up in materialistic pursuits?
- What family or cause might you be able to donate to if you cut back on spending?

Pursue: For a deeper dive, study 1 Timothy 6:6–19.

Father, you've blessed me in so many ways, and I thank you. This Christmas, help me use my wealth to bless others who are less fortunate than I am.

Shepherds on Motorcycles

It's such a serene picture: Mary, Joseph, and shepherds gazing adoringly at the babe in the manger—a tiny lamb wrapped around each shepherd's shoulders. So heartwarming. An Instagram moment if there ever was one.

But first-century folks may have taken a different view of the shepherds' presence on that holy night. Many historians agree that in Christ's time, shepherds were marginal figures in society. They stood ready for a fight, armed to protect their flock, and often transient. In many cases, shepherds were regarded as dishonest thieves—guilty until proven innocent. Some have compared them to the modern-day equivalent of motorcycle gangs.[8] While the shepherds around Bethlehem most likely raised lambs for Passover sacrifices, they were a far cry from model citizens.[9]

You can't help but wonder why God would choose outlaws to be the first witnesses (other than Mary and Joseph) of his Son's entrance into our world. This is a great question. In fact, the same query could be posed over nearly every detail of the Christmas story. Why choose a young teenage peasant to give birth to the Messiah? Why select a working-class tradesman as the man to raise him? Why would Jesus's parents live in such an obscure village that someone asked, "Can any good thing come out of Nazareth?" (John 1:46)?

Why be born in a barn with a bunch of smelly animals in the delivery room? Why was the Son of God wrapped in rags? Why would he be placed in a feeding trough? Why? Why? Why? These questions pose a plethora of possibilities: perhaps to demonstrate his humility, perhaps to prove how far God is willing to go in his love for us, perhaps to show he could relate to even the lowliest of men. Or perhaps all of the above.

The answer to each question is the same: "We don't know." Even if portions of the story seem foolish to us, God knows what he's doing. (He is the almighty, all-seeing, all-knowing Creator, after all). In Isaiah 55:8–9 we read, "The LORD says: 'My thoughts and my ways are not like yours. Just as the heavens are higher than the earth, my thoughts and my ways are higher than yours'" (CEV). God certainly doesn't do things the way we would—at the manger or in every day of our lives. We can all be thankful for this.

Principle

God's ways are not our ways.

Ponder

- In what area of your life do you struggle most with your ways being different from God's?
- How can you develop a more trusting and submissive spirit in this area?

Pursue: For a deeper dive, study Isaiah 55:6–13.

Lord, grant me a heart that trusts you more, especially in those areas of life that don't make sense.

"I Hate Christmas"

My friend (let's just call him Joe) hates Christmas. "Once Thanksgiving arrives, I count the days until the new year. I can't wait for Christmas to be over," he complains.

"What do you hate so much about Christmas?" I ask.

"Everything! Traffic, crowds, expenses, feeling obligated to buy gifts for people I barely know." Just to clarify, Joe pretty much doesn't like people in general.

From Thanksgiving through New Year's Day, we leave Joe alone to simmer in his Scrooge stew. Then, once January 2 rolls around, Joe returns to his sunny, delightful self—if this is even remotely possible.

Joe doesn't have a wife or kids—thank the Lord—so on one level, I get it. Christmas *is* hectic. It *is* expensive. And it *can* be a headache. But Joe's missing something huge. Christmas is filled with blessings: family, friends, nostalgia, Christmas spirit. Even the chaos of the crowds can be fun, if seen as a once-a-year adventure. But viewing Christmas through the lens of holiday hassles? This is a sad way to live.

Consider the chaos of the first Christmas. Besides facing the scorn of their village, Mary and Joseph endured a five-day journey to Bethlehem, with pregnant Mary probably bouncing on a donkey. When they arrived, all the inns were full. (No Hotels.com in those days.) So God's Son was literally born in a barn.

Later that night, a bunch of smelly shepherds ventured down from the hills to worship him—enough to scare the holiness out of even the most spiritually hardy. Then throw in the little drummer boy. Who needs some kid pounding on a drum right after you've given birth? (Okay, relax, I know he's not in the Bible.) Then the family fled to Egypt, barely escaping the swords of Herod's soldiers. Kind of puts the kibosh on our whining over Christmas traffic.

If we adopt a Joe-like attitude, holiday hassles can squelch our Christmas spirit quicker than we can say, "Ho, ho, ho." But before allowing Christmas chaos to throw cold eggnog on our Yuletide cheer, pause and consider the Christmas story. Stepping back and contemplating the big picture can change our perspective big time.

The next time we feel overwhelmed by the chaos of Christmas, take a deep breath, look up, and thank God for holiday hassles—and pray for people like Joe.

Principle

Don't allow the chaos of Christmas to steal your holiday joy.

Ponder

- What's the most stressful, chaotic aspect of the holidays?
- Which facet of the Christmas story calms your spirit?

Pursue: For a deeper dive, study Matthew 6:19–34.

Father, thank you for the joys and chaos of the Christmas season.
Even in the midst of holiday stress, help me discover your blessings.

Jesus and the SEALs

A team of Navy SEALs stormed a building to rescue a group of American hostages held in an enemy compound. They kicked in the door where the captives sat curled up in a corner, terrified. One of the SEALs shouted, "Get up and follow us! Hurry!" But the prisoners, frozen in terror, refused to budge. They didn't believe their rescuers were really Americans.

One of the team members put down his weapon, took off his helmet, and sat down on the floor next to the hostages. He softened the look on his face and put his arms around the captives. He wanted them to know he was one of them. He remained there until some of the prisoners made eye contact. The Navy SEAL whispered, "We're Americans. We've been sent to rescue you." The soldier stood to his feet, and one of the hostages did the same, then another, until all were willing to go. The story ended with all the hostages safe on American soil.[10]

It doesn't take a spiritual Einstein to see the parallel. We're the captives, and Jesus is our deliverer. It's simple. It's profound. It's breathtaking. The Son of God kicked in the door of our sinful world, breaking through the compound of darkness where Satan held us captive. When Jesus was born, God took off his helmet, set aside his weapon, and sat down next to us. He whispered, "I'm here to save you."

But like the hostages, we find it hard to trust him. At some point in our lives, most of us have experienced an unhealthy fear of God. Satan attempts to convince us God doesn't have our best interests at heart. But Jesus annihilates these concerns forever. First John 4:18 states, "There is no fear in love. But perfect love drives out fear."

The Navy SEAL's behavior was brave and beautiful, but a mere reflection of God's actions two thousand years ago. In Bethlehem, God broke down every barrier and removed every unhealthy fear to demonstrate he was our rescuer. He put his arms around us and whispered, "I'm one of you, and I'm here to save you." Christmas shows us that when we question God's motives, we need to look to the manger—because no one's afraid of a baby.

Principle

In Bethlehem, God broke down the barriers between us and removed our fears.

Ponder

- In what ways does the story of the Navy SEAL impact you?
- How can looking to the manger help release your unhealthy fears of God?

Pursue: For a deeper dive, study 1 John 4:7–18.

Lord, thank you for kicking in the door of my captivity and setting me free. Thank you for showing me I can trust you.

O Come, Emmanuel

My classmates and I were singing Christmas carols in the second grade when an inexpressible emotion welled up within me. Although I couldn't identify this penetrating passion that caused me to tear up, I knew there was more to Christmas than Santa Claus and reindeer.

Ditto for my wife. When Linda was three years old, her mom placed a tiny nativity in her room. Even though her parents weren't believers, Linda fell in love with Jesus through that nativity.

Deep within our souls lies a longing—a longing so intense words can't express it. This craving is rooted in the essence of who we are—created in the image of God with a hunger for more of him. Consider these thoughts from the Psalms: "As the deer pants for streams of water, so my soul pants for you, my God" (42:1). "I thirst for you, my whole being longs for you" (63:1). "My heart and my flesh cry out for the living God" (84:2). "My soul faints with longing for your salvation" (119:81).

Christmas carols speak to this longing. When we sing "O come, O come, Emmanuel, and ransom captive Israel, that mourns in lonely exile here, until the Son of God appear," our hearts identify with Israel's cry as they languished in captivity. We too cry out for Emmanuel our Savior to invade our lives and deliver us from exile on this planet. The origins of this carol have roots in the Gregorian Benedictine chants from the late eighth century AD, indicating that this passionate longing has persisted for dozens of generations.[11]

In a sense, every longing we have is a longing for God. Bruce Marshall in *The World, the Flesh and Father Smith*, wrote, "The young man who rings the bell at the brothel is unconsciously looking for God."[12] We're all seeking the love and freedom God offers. Satan distorts this search, the world co-opts it, and our flesh twists it, but the core of our craving reveals a longing for God. Words cannot express this secret whisper from God—like trying to describe a sunset to someone born blind.

More than at any other time, we experience this longing during Christmas—as I did in the second grade. It's what Christmas is all about. Far greater than nostalgia, it calls forth the heartfelt desperation for hope beyond life as it now exists. Adam and Eve's fall in Eden stole something from us. Christmas restores it. Like ancient Israel, our hearts cry out, "O come, Emmanuel."

Principle

During Christmas, we experience a deep longing for hope beyond life as we know it now.

Ponder

- In what ways or situations do you identify this longing in your heart?
- What Christmas customs or practices help bring out your longing for God?

Pursue: For a deeper dive, study Psalm 84.

> *Lord God, deep within my soul I long for you. I don't totally understand it. In the midst of this hectic season, speak to my heart and help me to hear your voice.*

Down on Your Knees

In 1999, Linda and I visited the Church of the Nativity in Bethlehem, the traditional site of Christ's birth. We were awestruck by the ornate fabrics and gold filigree adorning the walls. The aroma of incense floated through the air as long-robed priests waved their censers in reverential splendor. A gold star embedded in the marble floor marked the supposed spot where Mary gave birth. As beautiful as the church is, I'm guessing the simple stable, carved in limestone, where two Jewish peasants spent the night two thousand years ago probably didn't have marble floors.

Our guide led us down a set of stairs beneath the opulent edifice to a dark cave over which the church is built. This humble place bears little resemblance to the magnificent structure above it, but is a much more realistic picture of the place Jesus was born. We marveled at its simplicity and couldn't miss the symbolism.

The opening to the cave was so low that we couldn't walk in. We knelt, then inched forward. Whoever entered the stable the night Christ was born most likely had to do so on their knees. This still holds true today. To approach Jesus, we must kneel and humble ourselves before him. God isn't impressed by what impresses us. He's far more affected by a humble heart. In *The Applause of Heaven*, Max Lucado writes, "You can see the world standing tall, but to witness the Savior, you have to get on your knees."[13]

We've made an industry out of idolizing external glamor, but we often miss the magnitude of humility. Throughout his life, our Lord embodied this trait. The one time he described his personality, Jesus said, "I am gentle and humble in heart" (Matthew 11:29). Rather than clamoring for greatness, let's imitate his humility.

Pride is the only infirmity that sickens others rather than the one afflicted with it. We're blind to this malady, but others can spot it in a second, like a neon sign flashing over our heads. In contrast, we need to live on our knees—in service to God and others. Far from merely posturing ourselves physically, kneeling is a condition of the heart.

Throughout this holiday season, let's honor God's greatness with our lives. Let's acknowledge that we're not "all that." And let's approach God on our knees.

Principle

To approach Jesus, we must kneel.

Ponder

- In what areas of your life do you struggle with humility?
- What steps can you take to guard yourself against pride and embrace humility?

Pursue: For a deeper dive, study James 4:5–10.

Lord Jesus, thank you for your example of humility. Open my eyes to see areas of pride which prevent me from approaching you on my knees.

Wise Men Still Seek Him

Hopefully, this bit of news won't burst anyone's nativity bubble. The Wise Men are *not* part of the Christmas story. Despite the pictures, traditions, and nativity scenes, the Magi weren't there. They didn't come until sometime later. Matthew 2:11 records them visiting Jesus in "the house," not the stable. The traditional date for their visit is January 6, the source of the Twelve Days of Christmas—the days between Christmas and Epiphany.

But wait . . . there's more. Nowhere does Scripture tell us there were *three* of these visitors from the east. It's mere tradition that men named Gaspar, Balthasar, and Melchior graced the stable with their presence. The Magi brought three gifts, so I suppose we assume there were three wise men. Perhaps this is a safe assumption. I can't imagine showing up to the Messiah's baby shower without a gift.

As long as I'm dismantling Magi myths, these men weren't kings, either. The Magi were most likely uber-advanced scholars from Persia. They studied stars, ancient documents, and dreams. One writer called them the "Jedi knights of the ancient world."[14]

But before we toss the Magi from our nativity sets, does it really matter? Probably not. But this does matter: these guys journeyed hundreds of miles for months on end to glimpse Deity in diapers. They possessed a passionate spiritual hunger which drove them to pursue Truth in human form. They weren't Jews, but God honored their desire to seek him and know his physical manifestation, even if he was a mere babe.

Isn't this what God desires of us this Christmas? Christmas trees, Santa Claus, and Rudolph are all fine. But while we're buried in tinsel and lights, let's not abandon the message of the Magi. Christmas is about seeking Jesus. Christmas is about pursuing the deepest desire of our heart: to know him. Christmas is the time when an infinite God made himself finite. A time when the Immortal One embraced our mortality. When the Almighty God manifested himself as a weak, helpless infant.

Whether three or twenty Magi visited the manger or whether they came to a stable or a house, they sought Jesus. He invites us to do the same. In the midst of all the distractions, let's not neglect what really does matter. As the adage goes, "Wise men still seek him." May each of us find ourselves to be wise men and women this Christmas.

Principle

God desires that each of us seek Christ this Christmas.

Ponder

- On a scale of one to ten, how passionately are you pursuing Jesus?
- As you focus on the Magi, what steps can you take to rise above the superficial and seek the significant?

Pursue: For a deeper dive, study Matthew 2:1–12.

Lord, I'm so easily distracted by the glitter of the holidays.
Help me remember to seek you at Christmas.

The Messiah's Misfits

"Rudolph the Red-Nosed Reindeer" began as a promotional gimmick and ultimately resulted in the world's number-two selling Christmas song. In 1939, advertising executive Robert May wrote a poem for a department store sales campaign. It debuted that year in a booklet published by the Montgomery Ward chain of stores. More than 2.5 million copies were distributed to children. By 1946 the total had reached over 6 million. Singing cowboy Gene Autry recorded the song in 1949, increasing Rudolph's popularity. The tune's acclaim skyrocketed in 1964, when NBC transformed it into the popular animated television classic.

Today, "Rudolph the Red-Nosed Reindeer" has sold more than 25 million copies, second only to "White Christmas" in sales of holiday songs. The tune has been recorded hundreds of times and is listed in the top-twenty money earners in the history of the American recording industry.[15]

How do we explain the continued popularity of a fictional, flawed caribou? (Random Christmas fact: caribou and reindeer are the same species.) I believe it's the basic message of grace. The 1964 cartoon depicts Rudolph and his friends as misfits. Although a misfit, his bright, shining defect enabled Santa to deliver his toys "one foggy Christmas Eve."

Isn't this how God loves to operate? To work wonders through our weaknesses. First Corinthians 4:10 reads, "We're the Messiah's misfits" (MSG). When Jesus chose his original followers, he didn't select the brightest and best. He chose a bunch of misfits—for the most part common folks, such as fishermen and tax collectors.

Often it's our weaknesses that glorify God most. The Lord told Paul, "My power is made perfect in weakness," causing the apostle to exclaim, "When I am weak, then I am strong" (2 Corinthians 12:9–10). Isn't this the message of the manger—God making himself weak?

Our mistakes mold our ministry. Our failures form our fruitfulness. Think about it. Who ministers most capably to addicts? Addicts in recovery. Who can best serve the needs of the divorced than those who have experienced the grief of divorce. Many of those considered misfits by culture are the very ones God works through most powerfully to heal the hurting around us. He transforms our tragedies into triumphs. Let's celebrate our weaknesses. Let's delight in our defects. Then watch God use them for his glory. Like Paul. Like Rudolph. Like me.

Let's proudly proclaim, "We are the Messiah's misfits."

Principle

God loves to use our defects for his glory.

Ponder

- What weaknesses do you have that God might shape into a ministry?
- How can you make yourself available to God so he can use your weaknesses?

Pursue: For a deeper dive, study 2 Corinthians 12:1–10.

Dear Lord, thank you for my weaknesses, many of which glorify you. Instead of being ashamed of them, help me to embrace them.

A Father for God

Imagine God assigned you the task of choosing the man who would raise the Son of God. I'd start by making a list of his essential qualities. Wealth would be critical. He'd need a bushel of bucks to provide a comfortable lifestyle for the Great I Am. Certainly prominence and position to promote God's arrival into our world. Unquestionably, a religious leader—a member of the Jewish ruling council.

But God flips our priorities on their head. He esteems character qualities far above the superficial values we cherish. God selected a man of courage willing to face the whispers, the finger-pointing, the nose-in-the-air looks as he and Mary walked by.

God chose a man willing to trust him and step out in obedience, even when it turned his life topsy-turvy. And don't forget compassion. Only a tenderhearted man is willing to show mercy to a woman he's convinced has betrayed him.

In short, a man like Joseph of Nazareth. We know little about Joseph. He possessed no prosperity, position, or prominence—he was just a lowly carpenter from an off-the-beaten-path village.

He was a man of few words. So few we won't find a single quote from Joseph in Scripture. Comments abound from every other character in the story—Mary, Zechariah, Elizabeth, Herod, angels, shepherds, and Magi. But when it comes to Joseph? Silence. In fact, in the entire Bible, I can't think of a more significant character who uttered no recorded words. Even Balaam's donkey scored a few lines in Scripture.

Joseph may have been the strong, silent type, but his actions speak volumes. He took God at his word and married Mary. He risked a five-day journey to Bethlehem so his son could be born in the city of

David. He stood in the background, shooing away the animals while Mary was in labor.

He listened to God—much more than he talked. Four times in the story, God communicated to Joseph in dreams. God spoke . . . and Joseph obeyed.

Courage, compassion, humility—that's what God values. We can learn a lot from Joseph, who was considered inconsequential in his day but viewed as a spiritual giant today. Clearly, God chose the perfect man for the job: Joseph, a son of David and father to the Son of God.

Principle

God esteems character qualities far above the superficial values we cherish.

Ponder

- Which of Joseph's qualities do you admire most: courage, compassion, or humility? Why?
- Which of these do you need to work on most? What step will you take toward that goal?

Pursue: For a deeper dive, study Matthew 1:18–25.

Father, thank you for choosing a man like Joseph to raise your Son. Help me rise to the level of courage, humility, and compassion that he exhibited.

Listen for the Chimes

Erma Bombeck wrote of the legend of a church where chimes rang miraculously whenever someone gave a heartfelt, sacrificial gift. But the chimes hadn't rung for a long time, even when wealthy patrons made enormous donations. Then one Christmas Eve, a peasant boy knelt before the altar. Seeing baby Jesus, he took off his tattered coat and laid it on the manger. The chimes rang out.

Don't you love it when you hear the chimes? And aren't you surprised by the little things that open your heart to hear them? When our church found out about a family who had experienced a serious financial setback, several members purchased gifts and a tree. They quietly deposited them on the family's porch, rang the doorbell, and scattered. I heard the chimes that night.

Sacrificial giving doesn't necessitate a financial outlay. In O. Henry's classic short story "The Gift of the Magi" a young couple who had no money for Christmas gifts sold their prized possessions to buy each other presents. Della sold her hair to a wigmaker to purchase a chain for her husband's watch. Meanwhile, Jim sold his watch to buy ornamental hair combs for Della. Over a century later, we can still hear the chimes ring from such sacrificial giving.

But to hear the chimes, we have to be listening. They come in forms we don't easily recognize. My wife loved decorating our home and created magic every holiday season. The first Christmas after she died, my eleven-year-old granddaughter strung lights and garlands all over the house, and helped me decorate our tree, without being asked. I not only heard the chimes, but to this day, I cry tears of joy, thinking of Olive's sacrificial giving.

God loves to bring forth the spectacular from the ordinary. First Corinthians 2:9 reads, "'What no eye has seen, what no ear has heard, and what no human mind has conceived'—the things God has prepared for those who love him." This includes every aspect of the Christmas story. When Jesus was born, chimes rang like crazy. But few were listening. Anticipate the chimes. Expect them. Listen for them. And get ready for the wonderful surprises God has in store.

Principle

Look and listen for ways we can make the chimes ring through our heartfelt sacrificial giving.

Ponder

- When have you heard the chimes ringing at Christmas?
- How can you prepare yourself and your family to practice sacrificial giving in everyday events?

Pursue: For a deeper dive, study 1 Corinthians 2:6–16.

*Lord, thank you for the times you ring the chimes in my life—
when you bring the spectacular out of the ordinary. Help
me to listen for them and appreciate those moments.*

A Christmas Lamb

Christmas Eve, 2011. An on-duty watchman stands guard at a live nativity display at the Krohn Conservatory in Cincinnati. A baby lamb's cry interrupts the silence, as the wooly infant enters the world. A lamb born on Christmas Eve in a stable. The birth went well with no complications. The lamb's owner settled on a name . . . Mary Christmas.

Okay, it's not a stop-the-presses, read-all-about-it story. But it's still pretty amazing. It parallels a two-thousand-year-old event, when the Lamb of God entered our world in a stable. We don't know the exact date of Jesus's birth, but don't miss the comparison. A lamb born in a nativity on the eve before we celebrate the birth of the Lamb of God. How cool is that?

In John 1:29 John the Baptizer points to Jesus and says, "Look, the Lamb of God, who takes away the sin of the world!" John wasn't running around randomly shouting out animal names at passersby—such as "You're an aardvark." Any Jew listening to John would have instantly understood the lamb metaphor. After offering sacrificial lambs for hundreds of years, their excitement level would have skyrocketed. The authentic Lamb of God, the long-awaited Messiah, had come! One of John's disciples, Andrew, was so overcome with exuberance that he ran home, grabbed his brother Peter, and dragged him to see Jesus.

Jesus, the Lamb God—isn't this the Easter story? Yes, but the two stories are connected. Whether we speak of the manger, the cross, or the empty tomb, these three images are, like a tangled vine, impossible to separate. In a sense, Jesus was born to die. The precious Lamb of God.

From eternity, God saw you and wanted to be with you. First Peter 1:19–20 speaks of Jesus as "a lamb without blemish or defect. He was chosen before the creation of the world, but was revealed in these last times for your sake." For your sake. This is why heaven's hosts said goodbye to the Son. This is why Jesus was born. The phrase "Lamb of God" is much more than a catchy phrase on a Christmas card. It reveals God's heart. He longed for you to be with him so much that he sent his Son to earth. Jesus, the Lamb of God, born in a stable on Christmas day, to be sacrificed for us all.

Principle

Jesus, the Lamb of God, was born and sacrificed so you could live with God forever.

Ponder

- In what ways does Christmas remind you not only of Christ's birth but also his life and death?
- How can you discover new ways to appreciate his sacrifice for you during this holiday season?

Pursue: For a deeper dive, study 1 Peter 1:18–21.

Precious Lamb of God, words cannot express my love and gratitude for your sacrifice for me. I praise you and thank you for your indescribable love.

A Hidden Christmas Letter

O n December 24, 1961, Robert Crampton of Worksop, England, composed a letter to Santa. He tossed it in the fire, customary for kids in Britain, so it would float up and reach Father Christmas at the North Pole. Robert asked for a "cowboy suit and guns and a hat and everything," stating that would be "enough" for him for Christmas. The letter was marked "urgent," with a postscript, "See you tomorrow night."

In 2021, a chimney sweep service discovered the letter stuck in the chimney of Crampton's childhood home—sooty but still intact after sixty years. Spokesperson Cheryl Thorne stated, "It's a chimney treasure—it's precious when you find something like this."[16]

In our cynical age, when news reports ooze with stories of entitlement and victimhood, isn't it heartwarming to read a young boy's humble Christmas list from six decades past? He even unselfishly stated that those few presents would be "enough."

It's also refreshing to consider how often Christmas blessings come from surprising places. A letter discovered in a chimney after sixty years. Or a child's exuberant shout after receiving a gift he didn't expect. Or a divine gift found in a manger by humble shepherds.

In Matthew 7:7 Jesus said, "Ask and it will be given to you; seek and you will find; knock and the door will be opened to you." Jesus wasn't speaking of Father Christmas. That promise comes from no other than our heavenly Father, Creator of the universe.

In theory, Santa blesses every good little boy and girl, granting their requests. But God does something even greater. He loves us enough to sometimes say, "No, for now," when we're not ready for some of his blessings. Thank God for this. If the Lord gave me everything I asked for, I'd be dead.

God's timing is always perfect, but it might take sixty years to answer some of our requests—and answers may come in ways we didn't expect. It's so hard to wait. Zechariah and Elizabeth waited decades before God finally answered their prayers with the birth of baby John (Luke 1:13).

So it is with our letters to God. Our prayers always reach him . . . and he goes to work answering them immediately. But don't worry. None of our requests will ever remain stuck in the chimney for sixty years.

Principle

God answers our prayers, but his responses may not come when or how we expect.

Ponder

- When have you been surprised by how God answered one of your prayers?
- How can you learn to trust him during the times you are disappointed?

Pursue: For a deeper dive, study Matthew 7:7–11.

Heavenly Father, once again I surrender to your will. I trust that you'll always answer my prayers in the very best way possible, because I know you truly love me and only want what's good for me.

The Trouble with Chickens

The trouble with chickens is they're so . . . chicken. Ever try to catch one? Good luck. You'll quickly exhaust yourself as they run from you like a bunch of . . . chickens. Living in the country, Linda and I possess a flock of these panicky poultry. Occasionally, a hen breaks free from her pen to dine on bugs in our yard. It's a treat for her, but poses a deadly threat, since chicken-eating foxes and raccoons dwell all around us.

Recently, a hen escaped, and I zigzagged all over the yard attempting to catch her. Eventually I succeeded, but not without great frustration. (Try not to enjoy picturing this.) If only she knew how much I desired her best interest, I thought, she wouldn't flee from me in terror. If only she knew my heart for her—my true nature—she'd know she doesn't need to fear me. As bizarre as it sounds, it even occurred to me that if I could somehow become a chicken, I could show her that I have no desire to harm our little flock.

Isn't this exactly what Jesus did for us? Isn't this the message of Christmas? Philippians 2:5–8 declares that Jesus was equal to God. He left heaven, was born as a baby, and ultimately died a tortuous death, demonstrating the depth of his love for us. But to accomplish this, God had to become a "chicken."

Jesus also came to earth to show us God's true nature—what he's really like. In John 14:9 Jesus states, "Anyone who has seen me has seen the Father." I confess, at times I struggle to understand God. (Can I get a witness?) Even after years of studying the Bible, I read portions of the Old Testament and occasionally say to myself, "I just don't get God." But I do get Jesus.

God came down so we could see his true nature—what love looks like in human form. In this season of celebrating God's incarnation, perhaps this silly chicken story will help us appreciate his love. Never doubt God's intentions for us. Jesus reveals God's heart for his flock and his love for us. He only desires the best for us, even when we act like a bunch of chickens.

Principle

One reason God became man is to demonstrate his loving nature toward us.

Ponder

- What aspect of God's nature in Scripture do you most struggle to understand?
- How does his incarnation help you understand him better?

Pursue: For a deeper dive, study Luke 4:14–21.

Lord Jesus, my nature is to fear what I don't understand. During this season, help me focus on you and appreciate your deep love for me.

Christmas at the Hanoi Hilton

Captain Eugene McDaniel spent six grueling years in the infamous Hanoi Hilton, a brutal prison camp in Vietnam. Yet he experienced moments of pure joy. In his book *Scars and Stripes*, he describes the prisoners' Christmas celebrations. Each year, the fifty-seven men in the compound organized a program for Christmas week. One night someone shared a Christmas miracle story. Another man told the story of Ebenezer Scrooge in *A Christmas Carol*. Some conducted Christmas plays. They even had a choir. On Christmas Eve, McDaniel delivered a message.

For their Christmas tree, prisoners fashioned their olive-green socks into the shape of a tree and decorated it with bits of paper. On Christmas morning, prisoners distributed gifts. A man who didn't smoke gave cigarettes to one who did. The smoker shared candy with another.

McDaniel writes, "I couldn't express the beauty of those Christmases, the sharing of the little things we had . . . and to see each man's eyes light up, the smile come on his face . . . the profound simplicity which made it so beautiful. I don't know of any other Christmases that have meant more to me."[17]

While others spent thousands of dollars on gifts and decorations, these men battled starvation. Maybe we're missing something. Whether it's Christmas Day, New Year's Day, or Arbor Day, our joy has nothing to do with what we have or don't have.

Languishing in a Roman prison, Paul wrote, "I have learned to be content whatever the circumstances. I know what it is to be in need, and I know what it is to have plenty. I have learned the secret of being content in any and every situation" (Philippians 4:11–12).

Perhaps we need to learn the secret of contentment. Like Eugene McDaniel, Paul had every earthly reason to be miserable . . . but every heavenly reason to rejoice. So what's the secret? Are you ready? Practice gratitude for everything God gives you. Everything—even prison. That's it? Yup. It's so simple . . . and so hard. This is why Paul said he *learned* the secret.

Mary and Joseph had next to nothing as they lay exhausted in that stable. But I guarantee you no one on earth had more joy that night than that mother and father with their newborn child. Eugene McDaniel and his fellow prisoners mirrored this type of joy decades ago at the Hanoi Hilton.

Principle

Christmas joy has nothing to do with what we have or don't have.

Ponder

- When have you discovered real joy at Christmas, which had nothing to do with material things?
- How can you make Christmas simpler but more blessed this year?

Pursue: For a deeper dive, study Philippians 4:10–19.

Lord, thank you for inspiring stories such as Eugene McDaniel's. Help me appreciate the profound depth of simple gratitude during the holidays.

The Voice of Angels

On August 16, 1858, after laying the first transatlantic cable connecting North America with Britain, supervisors struggled to select the perfect words for the first official message sent via cable. Although dozens of test messages had been privately transmitted, when the time arrived to convey a public message via wire, they chose words from a Bible verse to capture the magnitude of this historic event: "Glory to God in the highest, and on earth peace, good will toward men" (Luke 2:14 KJV).

Of all messages the supervisors could have composed, they picked the words the angels proclaimed when Jesus was born. It was fitting. Like the birth of Christ, the transatlantic cable was a huge milestone in human history. But this is where the parallel ends. Comparing the magnitude of these two events is like comparing an elephant to an ant.

Imagine you're an angel. You've served the Almighty and mortals for eons. Imagine delivering the good news to the world that God had broken through the barrier of humanity. How amazingly, incredibly, wonderfully fantastic. (Okay, no more superlatives.) No wonder innumerable hosts of angels packed the skies, singing the praises of God. Their words shook the foundation of the cosmos as well as the spiritual realm: "Glory to God in the highest."

Here's how Gene Edwards describes the event in *The Birth*:

> Soon the white-robed visitors had filled the entire pasture land. On they came. Innumerable. Now the hills surrounding the pastures were filled. And yet more came, until it seemed every inch of earth from

the hills surrounding Bethlehem to the outskirts of Jerusalem were filled with messengers from heaven. . . .

As the angels themselves began to take in the magnificence of this unprecedented sight, they each began to shout with uninhibited joy. Pandemonium and delight wed in an exquisite moment of rapture. The sound was like a roar of a thousand seas.[18]

Imagine the angels' joy in leading the greatest worship song in history. But that was only the beginning. God invites us to join in their celebration. Besides Christmas carols and Advent services, we can pause and praise God anytime and anywhere, as the angels did on that holy night. Under our breath or at the top of our lungs, let's echo their words: "Glory to God in the highest."

Principle

The angels' message to the shepherds was the greatest worship event in humankind's history.

Ponder

- In what ways and in what times, do you find yourself praising God, like the angels, for the birth of his Son?
- What practical steps can you take to increase your level of praise to God this holiday season?

Pursue: For a deeper dive, study Psalm 148.

Almighty God, I join the angels in celebrating and praising you for the birth of your Son. Like them, I declare, "Glory to God in the highest."

People Who Look Like Me

Late one night I popped into the grocery store for a gallon of milk. I grabbed my carton of 2 percent from the dairy case in a dimly lit corner of the store. As I clutched my milk, a shadow loomed over me. When I stepped back, a huge man reached in and took one as well. Tattoos covered his arms, and he sported a host of piercings in places I didn't think were pierceable.

He thrust his huge hand out. "I'm Mike."

"Barney," I squeaked.

I turned to walk away. He followed—closely. I wondered if my sojourn on earth was about to come to an abrupt halt. As I looked for possible escape routes, he spoke again. "You live near here?"

"Yes," I replied, intentionally vague. I wasn't in the mood to be stalked.

"Where ya work?"

"I'm a minister." Surely this would discourage further conversation.

A huge smile engulfed his face. "Really? Me too! I'm planting a church for people who look like me. Because people who look like me probably wouldn't go to your church."

My holier-than-thou judgment evaporated quicker than water vapor on the sun. He was right. Our community needed a scary-looking guy to plant a church to reach scary-looking people. We prayed together, embraced, and I safely exited Safeway.

This Christmas lesson probably stretches us more than we wish. Jesus was born, as my new friend said, for "people who look like me." In Luke 19:10 Jesus described his reason for coming into the world:

"The Son of Man came to seek and to save the lost." This is why Jesus was born—to rescue "people who look like me." All of us.

I'm ashamed to admit it, but just as I judged Tattoo Man, there's a good chance I'd have judged Mary, Joseph, and Jesus that night in Bethlehem. The Messiah isn't supposed to look like that or be born in such squalor. If I'd been there, I'd have looked at him and thought, *You really think he's gonna save the world?*

Maybe Jesus was born in an animal stable to dismantle our prejudices, break down our self-righteousness, and open our hearts to embrace "people who look like me." I'm glad God showed me how easily I judge others in a dimly lit corner of Safeway at midnight.

Principle

Jesus was born to save "people who look like me."

Ponder

- What type of people do you tend to misjudge?
- How can you open yourself up to allow God to break through these judgments?

Pursue: For a deeper dive, study the story of Zacchaeus in Luke 19:1–10.

Lord, forgive me for the times when I look down on people and judge them without even thinking about it. Please remind me you were born to rescue "people who look like me."

White Elephants

Most of us have received at least one white elephant gift, especially this time of year. A friend hands us a party invite with the words, "Bring a white elephant gift." Perhaps the first time you saw that statement, you shook your head wondering, "How am I going to lay my hands on one of those?" It's a weird term, to be sure. Dictionary.com defines *white elephant* as "a possession unwanted by the owner but difficult to dispose of."

Evidently this crazy phrase originated in ancient times, with the king of Siam. He devised a cruel way to disable a courtier who had fallen out of favor. The king sent a rare and wonderful gift—a live albino elephant. Because the animal was considered sacred, the recipient was duty-bound to feed and care for it. The elephant required an exorbitant amount of time, energy, and resources. Eventually, the king's courtier would wear himself out caring for this rare gift. What originated as a blessing became a bane.[19]

Our world is crammed full of white elephants. Urgent matters scream for our attention. Details distract us like a noisy siren. It's a battle. Ephesians 5:16 warns us to be "making the most of every opportunity because the days are evil."

Our spiritual enemy would love nothing more than to yank our attention away from Jesus by shoving a white elephant in our faces. These beasts can suck the joy out of our holidays faster than a car-wash vacuum. More than any other season, our calendars overflow with commitments. We don't wish to relegate Jesus to the role of a white elephant . . . but we do, even though we may not realize it. Especially during the holidays, we have the opportunity to draw closer to our Lord. Some commitments may simply require a "no" response. It's hard, but the alternative—filling our planners with secondary tasks—will prove even more wearisome long-term. Remember, besides God, family comes first.

Try this. Intentionally carve out time to reflect on the reason for the season. Set aside your gift-wrapping, grab a cup of eggnog, and calm your soul in front of the hearth. (Even a fake TV fireplace will work.) Meditate on God's greatest gift to humanity—the gift of himself as a baby. I promise you this: instead of wearying you like an albino pachyderm, he will strengthen your soul. Focusing on Jesus brings joy and peace. He's the opposite of a white elephant gift.

Principle

Don't allow the white elephants of the holiday season to steal your time and energy.

Ponder

- What white elephants in your life do you need to get rid of?
- What steps can you take to make that happen?

Pursue: For a deeper dive, study Ephesians 5:8–20.

> *Lord, I find I'm far too rushed during the Christmas season. Help me carve out time during this busy time of year to experience the joy of your birth.*

I'm Not Clarence

Remember sitting at the kitchen table, pencil in hand, scribbling a letter to Santa? One youngster composed this epistle to Saint Nick: "Dear Santa, three boys live in this house: Greg, Mike, and Clarence. Greg is good some of the time. Mike is good some of the time. Clarence is good ALL of the time . . . I am Clarence."[20]

We'd all like to pretend we're Clarence—never messing up, our names perpetually gracing Santa's good list. But deep inside we know we make the naughty list more often than we like to admit. I'm not Clarence. None of us are. Even Clarence isn't Clarence.

Romans 3:10 states, "There is no one righteous, not even one." This is why Jesus was born, lived a perfect life, and was crucified, assimilating the guilt of every human sin—because we're not Clarence (see 2 Corinthians 5:21).

One of the biggest burdens we drag through life is shame. The side effects are disastrous—robbing us of joy, creating all sorts of sickness and depression. We embrace a myriad of ways to try to rid our hearts of this burden. We run through life at breakneck speed, afraid if we slow down, we'll face our failures. We chase after addictions to numb our shame—drugs, sex, shopping, or religion. Or we lie to ourselves, hoping to convince everyone around us that we are Clarence.

It's sad because it's so unnecessary. Jesus invites us to receive the forgiveness he offers. We can't earn it, buy it, or check off enough religious boxes to deserve it. His grace is God's Christmas gift to humanity.

Thank God, Jesus is not Santa Claus. Remember as a kid, expelling superhuman effort during the month of December to make Santa's good list? That's a lot of pressure. Even for twenty-five days, I didn't do so well. As for January through November? I don't wanna talk about it. Our burdens lift when we realize our human efforts don't determine whether we can avoid God's naughty list.

More than ever, we need to remember that Jesus is our Savior. He came to lift us out of the darkness of this broken world and set us free. Otherwise, we're all in a heap of trouble. God's grace is more than sufficient. Jesus was born so we don't have to be Clarence.

Principle

Jesus sets us free from the sin and shame in our lives.

Ponder

- What memories of shame are crippling you?
- How can you be free from them?

Pursue: For a deeper dive, study Romans 6:15–23.

> *Dear God, thank you for your unmerited favor. Thank you for sending your Son into our world to pay for my sin so I don't have to live a perfect life. I receive your grace.*

No Vacancy

We were driving through Kansas around midnight with two small children. The hotels were filled in every town we passed through. Eventually, we spotted a sign flashing *Vacancy*. Approaching the office, I prayed the desk clerk hadn't forgotten to turn on the *No Vacancy* sign. In retrospect, perhaps we should have kept driving.

When I turned on the lights in the room, cockroaches scattered. The door didn't lock, which made me as nervous as a roadrunner on caffeine. The curtains were tattered, and the shower knob fell off in my hand. But we had reached a point of exhaustion and would have slept in a stable. I sympathized with Joseph and Mary—only their plight was much worse.

Joseph scrambled to find a room because Mary was about to deliver the Messiah. But all the neon signs in Bethlehem flashed *No Vacancy*. The biblical text simply reads, "She wrapped him snugly in strips of cloth and laid him in a manger, because there was no lodging available for them" (Luke 2:7 NLT).

The innkeeper gets a bad rap in the Christmas story. We shake our heads, uttering "Tsk, tsk." How could anyone be so selfish as to turn away baby Jesus? (Although in his defense, the innkeeper didn't know he was baby Jesus). He wasn't a bad guy—just busy. Maybe he was stressed because of the census crowds cramming the streets. Maybe he couldn't imagine stuffing one more body into his hotel. It was easier to hang out a *No Vacancy* sign. Had the innkeeper known he sent the Messiah out into the cold, perhaps he would have given someone else the boot.

Really, the innkeeper is no different from us. Consider the time-worn cliché, "Make room in your heart for Jesus." There's a reason it's a cliché. We're busy people—trying to cram a hundred hours of commitments into a fifty-hour box. This is especially true during Christmas. Crowded malls, crowded halls, crowded roads, and crowded abodes. In the hectic hurry, how can we possibly find room for Jesus?

Christmas isn't about gifts, parties, and food—although I love all these things. Remember the innkeeper. Remember another cliché: "Jesus is the reason for the season." Don't hang a *No Vacancy* sign over your life this Christmas.

Principle

Like the innkeeper, we often don't have room for Jesus.

Ponder

- On a scale of one to ten, how busy is your life during the holidays?
- During the hectic holiday rush, what creative ways can you find to make Jesus feel welcome in your home and heart?

Pursue: For a deeper dive, study Psalm 32:7–11.

> *Lord Jesus, as I rush through my days, forgive me for leaving you out of my life, especially during the holidays. Forgive me for the times I make busyness an idol.*

"The Lord God Omnipotent Reigneth"

In 1741, George Frideric Handel wandered the streets of London angry at life. He reflected on a time when he enjoyed the applause of royalty. Envy at the success of others ate at his soul. Years earlier, a cerebral hemorrhage had afflicted the old composer, and he had only recently recovered from partial paralysis.

His staunch supporter, Queen Caroline, was dead. England had fallen on hard economic times. Heating large auditoriums for concerts was banned, and his performances were canceled. He began to question God's goodness.

Then his destiny changed.

Charles Jennens, a wealthy patron of the arts, had written the text for an oratorio and believed Handel was the man to compose the music. As he read Jennens's words, Handel was filled with a sense of the presence of God. He picked up his pen, and the music flowed through him. In only a few weeks, Handel completed the entire composition.[21]

Handel's *Messiah* was so well received in London that when the "Hallelujah Chorus" was sung by the choir, King George II supposedly rose to his feet, a tradition that continues to this day. The "Hallelujah Chorus" touches something deep inside us, and we rise to our feet when we hear its majestic music.

But it was birthed by a man on the verge of despair.

The lyrics to the "Hallelujah Chorus" are based on texts from the book of Revelation, written by the exiled apostle John, who was also in a desperate situation. "Hallelujah! For the Lord God omnipotent reigneth" (19:6). "The kingdom of this world is become the kingdom of our Lord, and of his Christ . . . and he shall reign for ever and ever" (11:15). "King of kings! And Lord of lords!" (19:16). John understood and Handel learned that no situation is permanent in view of eternity, no matter how hopeless it appears or how despondent we feel. We trust in God's presence, promises, and provision. We draw strength from fellowship with our family and friends.

Reflecting on Handel's *Messiah*, Joseph McCabe wrote, "Never again are we to look at the stars, as we did when we were children, and wonder how far it is to God. . . . Our God is closer than our problems. . . . He is here, beside us, Emmanuel."[22]

More than any other time of year, Christmas is a season of hope. The apostle John and George Handel demonstrated this with their lives. "Hallelujah! For the Lord God omnipotent reigneth."

Principle

No adversity is permanent in view of eternity.

Ponder

- How does the history behind Handel's Messiah offer hope and encouragement to you?
- How do the words from the book of Revelation remind us of the hope we can experience at Christmas?

Pursue: For a deeper dive, study Revelation 19:1–8.

Hallelujah! Lord Jesus, you reign forever and ever.

Puppy Love

Author Max Lucado tells the story of a boy who spied a box of puppies in a pet store window. Stepping inside, he asked the owner, "How much are the puppies?" Learning the price, he headed out.

For the next two weeks, he mowed lawns, washed cars, and did extra chores. Finally, he returned and plopped a wad of crumpled bills on the counter. The owner counted them and said, "Okay, go pick out your puppy."

The boy immediately chose a dog with a limp foot. The owner told him, "No son, don't get that dog—he's crippled. He'll never be able to run, or jump, or play with you."

The lad persisted. "No, this is the puppy I want." As the boy exited the store, the owner noticed something, and suddenly, he understood. Protruding out of the boy's pant cuff was a brace. He was also crippled. Know why the boy wanted that puppy? He knew how it felt not to be able to run and jump and play as other kids did.[23]

Hebrews 4:15 says this about Jesus: "This High Priest of ours understands our weaknesses, for he faced all of the same testings we do, yet he did not sin" (NLT). Know how it feels to be betrayed, abandoned, and lied about? So does Jesus. Accused of horrible crimes and denied justice? Jesus was too. Know what it's like to be poor, homeless, and surrounded by people whose constant demands leave you bone-weary? Ditto for Jesus. No matter what we've been through, Jesus has experienced it.

He entered our world and made himself lame, taking on all our weaknesses, fears, and suffering. He chose a humble birth—to be wrapped in rags and laid in a manger. He selected two young peasants for his parents. In his sovereignty, he knew they'd flee Bethlehem to escape the wrath of a demented king. He entered our world and became one of us. Jesus knows how we feel.

Verse 16 adds, "So let us come boldly to the throne of our gracious God. There we will receive his mercy, and we will find grace to help us when we need it most." Someone in heaven knows how we feel, and when we need it most, we can approach him boldly for mercy. Not as a slave, cowering in terror, but as his child.

Principle

Jesus knows how we feel.

Ponder

- How does the fact that Jesus understands our weaknesses impact the way you live?
- Under what situations do you draw comfort from the truth that Jesus knows how you feel?

Pursue: For a deeper dive, study Hebrews 4:14–16.

Lord Jesus, thank you for entering our world and becoming like me. Thank you for going through everything I go through to identify with me. I worship you this Christmas for enduring all you endured for me.

Shooting Ourselves Down

In 1956, a Navy test pilot flying an F11F Tiger was struck by several rounds of ammunition and eventually crashed. Only later did the pilot learn he had shot himself down. He was traveling so fast, he outran the ammo he was firing. The Navy considered the incident a one-in-a-million fluke and was certain it would never happen again. But it occurred once more in 1973.[24]

Ever feel like that pilot? Moving through life at breakneck speed, we can easily shoot ourselves down. Meetings to attend, reports to finish, chores to be completed. Then the appliances mutiny, all breaking down at once. (I swear they're in cahoots.) Throw in the holidays—hanging lights, putting up the tree, running from store to store to find gifts your kids can't live without. We're busier than Santa on Christmas Eve, and we discarded "peace on earth" in line at Walmart. During the holidays, we're more uptight than a long-tailed cat in a room full of rocking chairs, and our digestive tract pays the price, along with those we love most. We shoot ourselves down.

The solution lies in two simple words: Stop it!

Paul wrote in Philippians 4:6–7, "Do not be anxious about anything, but in every situation, by prayer and petition, with thanksgiving, present your requests to God. And the peace of God, which transcends all understanding, will guard your hearts and your minds in Christ Jesus."

I take the first step toward this peace when I realize I'm never going to get all my stuff done. Important stuff. Ever find your to-do list is longer at the end of the day than when you started? Truthfully,

I'm addicted to productivity. But I'm learning it's an unending cycle. There's always more that needs to get done than time to do it.

Here's what helps me. At the beginning of each day, I compose my list, numbering my tasks in order of importance. I surrender the list to God and tackle number one until I've completed it or have gone as far as I can. Then I move on. It's a simple method, but it makes a world of difference.

Trying to do one more thing when we're exhausted is a recipe for hypertension. But surrendering our lists to God in prayer brings peace that transcends understanding. It's a lot better than shooting yourself down with your own ammo.

Principle

Surrendering our to-dos to God in prayer brings peace that transcends understanding.

Ponder

- What specific aspect of the holidays do you find most stressful?
- How can you find peace by surrendering it to God?

Pursue: For a deeper dive, study Philippians 4:4–9.

Lord God, you are in charge of all things, including my time. Help me surrender my tasks to you and experience joy throughout the holidays.

Waiting for the Messiah

Do you remember how long it took for Christmas to arrive when you were a child? The year dragged along like a slug on Prozac. During December, your family set up and decorated the tree. Then gifts magically appeared. You rummaged through the wrapped presents like a wild animal foraging for food. Finally, you spied it—a tag with your name. You agonized over what treasure lay beneath the paper. Perhaps your curiosity won the tug-of-war with your self-control, and you ventured a peek. The discovery may not have ruined Christmas, but it created a bit of a letdown on Christmas morning. Part of the magic of Christmas is the anticipation.

In January, a low-level gloom set in, covering you like a thick blanket. An entire year lay ahead, and the days dragged along.

I wonder if this is how Simeon felt as he awaited the Messiah. We know little about him, except "it had been revealed to him by the Holy Spirit that he would not die before he had seen the Lord's Messiah" (Luke 2:26). Day after day, he entered the temple—waiting, watching. We don't know how long he lingered in the sanctuary. Surely his curiosity far surpassed that of a child waiting for Christmas day.

When he arose each morning, I imagine he asked himself, "Will this be the day?" As each person hurried past, I picture him pondering, "Is this the one?" Imagine how the days dragged on as he awaited God's gift to humanity.

Then, in a moment, everything changed. The Holy Spirit nudged him. *There they are. That young couple with the baby. They're the ones. Their infant is the Messiah.* Imagine how Simeon's heart leapt with joy. Don't know about you, but I don't think I could have contained myself.

Simeon held baby Jesus and prophesied, "Sovereign Lord, as you have promised, you may now dismiss your servant in peace" (Luke 2:29).

God calls each of us, like Simeon, to wait for the Messiah. In the morning we wait for him to open our hearts to what he has for us this day. We wait for him to fill us with a deeper awareness of his presence. Ultimately, we wait for him to return and take us home to live with him forever.

Principle

Like Simeon, each day we wait for the Messiah to meet us.

Ponder

- On a scale of one to ten, how good are you at waiting?
- As you wait to meet God face-to-face, what do you most anticipate—his presence, his blessings, his promises, or something else?

Pursue: For a deeper dive, study Luke 2:25–35.

Jesus, Messiah, I wait each day to meet with you. Fill my heart with joy and a deeper awareness of your presence.

The King and the Maiden

Danish theologian Søren Kierkegaard tells a parable of a powerful king who rode through the countryside one day, catching a glimpse of a beautiful maiden singing as she worked. Captivated by her loveliness and her voice, the king often returned to her village. He was smitten with love for the girl, but his kingship presented a problem. He could command her to come to his palace and marry him, but would she truly love him or obey out of fear? Would she be enamored by a life of royalty rather than loving him for the man he was?

The king concocted a radical scheme. He laid aside his royal robes and golden crown. He renounced his throne, abandoned his palace, and moved into her village and lived as a peasant. He hoped the maiden could come to know and love him for who he was. Eventually he won her heart, and she declared her love for him. Only then did he reveal his identity as a king. He brought her to his palace, and the maiden was crowned as queen.[25]

This parable is more than a fairy tale—it parallels the incarnation of Jesus. The King of the universe loved us with an everlasting love (Jeremiah 31:3). He set aside his throne, left his heavenly kingdom, and entered our village (Philippians 2:5–8). John 1:14 reads, "The Word became flesh and blood, and moved into the neighborhood" (MSG). Rather than cower before him in fear, we can truly love him for who he is.

As Advent reveals, the King entered our world incognito as a baby and grew into a man. He woos us with his love. As we come to love him, he brings us to his home, and we reign with him (Ephesians 2:6). It's romantic. It's daring. It's inconceivable. And it reveals how much we mean to God. He's so enamored by us, so crazy in love with us, that he became one of us. He's willing to pay any price to have an intimate relationship with us.

As we celebrate Christmas, let's recall this story. Consider the price the King of the universe was willing to pay for you. Remember the daring move he made to have you forever as his bride.

Principle

Jesus was willing to give up everything to have you as his bride.

Ponder

- Put yourself in this story. What emotions does it evoke?
- As you reflect on your life, especially in this season, how can you demonstrate your gratitude to Jesus for his love?

Pursue: For a deeper dive, study John 1:1–18.

Lord Jesus, King of the universe, no words can express my gratitude for you entering our world and choosing me to reign with you as your bride. Help me live in gratitude each day.

Nuthin' A Tall

In 1918, H. T. Webster created a cartoon titled "Hardin County, 1809" honoring Abraham Lincoln's birthday. It depicts a supposed conversation between two locals on February 12, 1809:[26]

"Any news down t' th' village, Ezry?"

"Well, Squire McLean's gone t' Washin'ton t' see Madison swore in, an' ol' Spellman tells me this Bonaparte fella has captured most o' Spain. What's new out here, neighbor?"

"Nuthin' a tall. Nuthin' a tall, 'cept fer a new baby down t' Tom Lincoln's. Nuthin' ever happens out here."

Amazing. One of the greatest figures in American history is born, and it's viewed as "nuthin' a tall." But isn't this what we'd expect? I wonder if a similar conversation occurred in Bethlehem two-thousand years ago:

"Anything important happen here last night?"

"No, nuthin' a tall, 'cept over at the old innkeeper's stable. Seems some couple from way up north had a baby. Like I said, nuthin' a tall ever happens out here."

To outside observers, Jesus's birth was "nuthin' a tall." Hundreds of travelers crowded into a tiny berg to register for the census. During the night, a young woman gave birth to a baby. Sure, it was in a stable, but it's doubtful anyone else in Bethlehem even noticed (except the shepherds). If folks did take note, the event probably only warranted a ten-second conversation. But can you imagine the celebration occurring in heaven? Angels danced and partied like it was AD 1 (which, in fact, it was).

I wonder how often we miss the events that are important to God. In

Mark 12:41–44, Jesus sat in the temple treasury, watching wealthy people present their offerings. But who attracted his attention most? A poor widow who put in two pennies. No one else noticed her. The woman's contribution was "nuthin' a tall" from the other people's perspective.

Maybe you feel as if this is the story of your life. "What have I ever done? Nuthin' a tall." Maybe you taught Sunday school at church. What were you doing? Nuthin' . . . just planting seeds of God's Word in the hearts of future generations. Or maybe you served the homeless. Or set up chairs so a preacher could share God's Word. It might seem like "nuthin' a tall" to us. But what we see as nuthin' could turn out to be God's greatest work. Just like that night in Bethlehem, when an event that seemed like nuthin' changed the world forever.

Principle

What seems like nothing could be God's greatest work.

Ponder

- In what ways do you serve that you and others might consider unimportant?
- Ask God to open the eyes of your heart to see things from his perspective.

Pursue: For a deeper dive, study Mark 12:41–44.

Lord, thank you for using the small matters that often go unnoticed by the world but are of great significance to you. Open the eyes of my heart to see things through your eyes.

In the Shadow of the Herodian

Herod was not a nice guy. He butchered his brother, brother-in-law, father-in-law, his favorite wife, and two of his sons. Augustus Caesar stated, "It is better to be Herod's pig than son." Not exactly a candidate for Father of the Year.

But here's the clincher. Shortly before his death, Herod ordered soldiers to round up Judea's most distinguished citizens and execute them. He was concerned that no one would mourn his passing and wanted to make certain there would be sufficient lamenting. Fortunately, this demented order was not carried out.[27]

Add to these examples the massacre of Bethlehem's children, and the conclusion is obvious. Herod wasn't morally confused; he was downright evil. Evil beyond description. Matthew 2:16 records the heinous crime: "When Herod realized that he had been outwitted by the Magi, he was furious, and he gave orders to kill all the boys in Bethlehem and its vicinity who were two years old and under."

In the shadow of Herod's magnificent palace, the Herodian, lay the town of Bethlehem. Sleeping in his luxurious bed, Herod didn't have a clue that four miles away the King of Kings had been born to two peasants and was at that very moment lying in an animal feeding trough. This king would reign over heaven and earth—a ruler far more powerful than Herod. Even if Herod had known, he probably would have laughed before hunting the baby down to kill him. A king sleeping in a manger? That was nonsensical, like your crazy uncle claiming to be Napoleon. But that's exactly how it went down that night.

At the time of Jesus's birth, Herod's power was undisputed; his life-style, exceeded by none in the land; his influence, extensive. Infant Jesus had none of those qualities. He possessed nothing that makes for greatness in human terms.

But today? If it weren't for the biblical narrative, only a few history nerds would know Herod ever existed. The world tells us we find value in prosperity, power, and popularity. Jesus deconstructs those myths. Acknowledging God's power, Mary prophesied, "He has brought down rulers from their thrones but has lifted up the humble" (Luke 1:52). Two thousand years later, Herod's kingdom is rubble, but the kingdom ushered in by a helpless infant endures, growing and spreading faster than ever. We stand in awe of the power God displayed through a baby in a manger.

Principle

Herod illustrates that trusting in what the world offers is transitory and ultimately meaningless.

Ponder

- What does the comparison between Herod and Jesus teach you about trusting in what the world offers?
- What allurement of the world do you most struggle with: pride, pleasure, popularity, prominence, prosperity, or power?

Pursue: For a deeper dive, study Luke 12:13–21.

Lord, when I consider the world's system and Christ's kingdom, I realize the world has nothing to offer long-term. Help me remember this during times when the things of the world seize my heart.

God's Timing Is Perfect

On December 21, 2007, a Christmas card arrived at a home in Oberlin, Kansas. The card was mailed on December 23, 1914. Evidently, it was discovered somewhere in Illinois, where it was finally sent on its way. "It's a mystery where it spent most of the last century," Oberlin Postmaster Steve Schultz said.[28] At least the card arrived in time for Christmas–except that it was nearly a century too late.

In contrast, God's timing is always perfect. Before creating the universe, God developed a plan to save us (Ephesians 1:4). In the Old Testament, his purpose began to unfold. At the precise moment in history, when conditions were perfect, God's Christmas card arrived on our planet in the form of a baby. Galatians 4:4 reads, "When the set time had fully come, God sent his Son, born of a woman." God's timing is always perfect.

Seeing God work behind the scenes manipulating human actions to carry out his plan throughout history is fascinating. Everything converged at that one precise moment when Jesus was born. Consider this. Around 300 BC, Greece conquered the Mediterranean world and spread Greek language and culture. When Jesus was born, everyone in the region spoke one universal language (Koine Greek), enabling the gospel to be spread quickly. When Rome conquered Greece, they created a network of roads, making travel possible. They introduced Pax Romana, a form of so-called universal peace. The scene was set.

Shortly prior to Christ's birth, a general sense of expectancy filled the air, anticipating the coming of a great king. Historians such as Tacitus, Suetonius, and Josephus testify to a common belief that a king from Judea would arise and rule over the entire earth. The Magi's visit attests to this widespread premonition.

For centuries, the Jews had awaited the coming Messiah. In the midst of oppression, each generation cried out to God for deliverance. Finally, he came—in the fullness of time, when every condition was perfect.

Why is this important? Right now, each of us struggles with stressful situations—whether personal hardship or global unrest. We cry out to God, waiting for him to deliver us.

God knows what he's doing, and his timing is always perfect. He will act in "the fullness of time," just as he did when the Messiah was born. Although we may feel God has forgotten us, he hasn't. Wait on the Lord. He will move, at precisely the right moment—because God's timing is perfect.

Principle

God's timing is always perfect.

Ponder

- What struggles motivate you to cry out to God, asking him to resolve them?
- In what ways are you comforted by looking at history and seeing how God precisely orchestrated events for Jesus to come in the "fullness of time"?

Pursue: For a deeper dive, study Ephesians 1:3–14.

Almighty God, thank you for your perfect timing throughout the generations. Help me trust your perfect timing in my current struggles.

Home for the Holidays

We made the drive on I-90 West from Post Falls, Idaho, to Seattle, Washington, to celebrate Christmas with my in-laws so many times, I could do it in my sleep. Traveling with two small kids, I considered trying this on occasion, but my better judgment prevailed.

Only once in twelve years did we encounter a serious problem. Heavy snowdrifts covered Snoqualmie Pass. As we crested the summit, we were greeted by a semitruck jackknifed across all lanes. I slid off the road to avoid a collision. Glancing in the rearview mirror, I saw a car skidding backward toward us. He rear-ended us with his car's rear end. Seeing other vehicles about to do the same, Linda and I grabbed our kids and threw them to safety into a snowbank. We arrived in Seattle with a banged-up Buick, but we escaped serious harm.

"Home for the holidays." The phrase fills our heart with a myriad of memories. Some are beautiful. Some are as challenging as Santa squeezing down the chimney of a Fisher stove.

For me, a pleasant aroma of nostalgia arises when I recall those Christmas moments.

What insanity drives us to battle holiday traffic for hundreds of miles through weather fit only for sled dogs? What sort of craziness motivates normally sane people to stand for hours in airports, sleeping in an upright position, waiting for the next available seat because their flight was canceled? That nebulous entity we call home. It's not a place; it's a state of being.

Could these memories reflect a longing for our true home—heaven? Sitting by a warm fire, snow falling, surrounded by those we love is a tiny taste of eternal bliss. It's something we chase but can never quite catch in this world—because we weren't created for this world. We were created for heaven.

In John 14:2, Jesus paints this picture of being at home with him: "My Father's house has many rooms; if that were not so, would I have told you that I am going there to prepare a place for you?" Like a sweet dream we can't quite recall, like an itch just outside our reach, we dream of our real home. This is why we're driven by this crazy pursuit to go "home for the holidays."

Principle

Our longing to be home at Christmastime is actually a longing for our real home in heaven.

Ponder

- When do you find yourself homesick for heaven?
- What verses or sections of Scripture speak most profoundly to you of that longing?

Pursue: For a deeper dive, study Revelation 22.

Lord, thank you for the longing you have placed in me for heaven. Jesus, guide me to meditate more deeply on my future home with you.

D-Day and Christmas Day

Turning slowly, the stranger faced me as we stood at the drinking fountain. I thanked him through dewy eyes. As he wiped his tears, I knew he appreciated my gratitude. We embraced and departed, never to see one another again.

This memorable encounter happened in a theater, where I was watching *Saving Private Ryan*, which dramatized the events of June 6, 1944, D-Day, the beginning of the end of Hitler's tyranny. A total of two hundred thousand Allied troops perished in the Battle of Normandy, which began that stormy morning. I shudder, imagining the darkness we might live in today if those courageous soldiers hadn't stormed the beaches in northern France.

During the film, I was overcome with gratitude for their sacrifice. I silently promised God, "I'm going to thank the next vet I meet who fought on D-Day." At the film's end, I exited behind an older man. I overheard him tell an usher, "I fought there, at Omaha Beach, in Normandy."

I immediately sensed God's Spirit reminding me of my promise. "Not now, Lord. I'm an emotional wreck. I'll thank the next D-Day vet I meet."

He said to my heart, "You made a promise."

I've learned I don't win these arguments with the Lord, so I approached the man at the water fountain. I started to thank him, but the words caught in my throat. Eventually, I squeaked out my gratitude. The vet began to cry, thanked me, and we hugged. Even as I pen these words, my eyes fill with tears, recalling that moment.

Let's think about another D-Day: December 25 in AD 1—the traditional date of Christ's birth. In the most daring undercover operation in history, God entered our world disguised as an infant. He sneaked in behind enemy lines to deliver the human race from the prince of darkness. The enemy's opposition was fierce. Rome's census, a perilous journey to Bethlehem, no room at the inn, and, later, Herod's slaughter of innocent children—Satan's greatest efforts couldn't hinder God's battle plan. The Lord prevailed. Colossians 2:15 states, "He disarmed the spiritual rulers and authorities. He shamed them publicly by his victory over them" (NLT).

C. S. Lewis wrote, "Enemy-operated territory—that's what this world is. . . . The rightful king has landed . . . in disguise."[29]

If Jesus hadn't been born, we'd be doomed for eternity. Thank God he sent his Son, born to sacrifice his life and ultimately defeat mankind's spiritual enemy so we could experience freedom for now and all eternity.

Principle

Because of the birth, death, and resurrection of Jesus, we've been delivered from bondage for all eternity.

Ponder

- As we are touched by the soldiers' sacrifice on D-Day, how have you been touched by understanding the sacrifice Jesus made for you?
- In what ways can you show your gratitude to Jesus for his deliverance?

Pursue: For a deeper dive, study Colossians 2:9–15.

Dear Jesus, as grateful as we are for those who have sacrificed their lives for our freedom, we are overwhelmingly more grateful for your sacrifice in coming into our world to free us for eternity.

"I Heard the Bells on Christmas Day"

Christmas Day, 1863. America's poet laureate, Henry Wadsworth Longfellow, found himself battling deep depression. The United States was no longer united. It was embroiled in the Civil War, the country's bloodiest conflict. A devout abolitionist, his heart was broken by the horrific fighting. Even worse, his personal grief was overwhelming. A month earlier, his oldest son had been critically wounded in battle. Two years prior, his wife, Fannie, burned to death in front of him when her clothes caught fire. Longfellow was permanently injured attempting to extinguish the flames that enveloped her body.

Filled with despair, he looked out his window in Cambridge, Massachusetts. He ruminated on the angel's words to the shepherds in Luke 2:14—"Peace on earth, good will to men." He scoffed, "There is no peace on earth."[30]

Perhaps Longfellow wondered if these tragic events mocked God's promise of peace.

Then church bells began to ring. What followed can only be described as a Christmas miracle. Longfellow's spiritual eyes were opened, and his perspective on the world changed. The great poet penned these words:

> I heard the bells on Christmas Day, their old,
>   familiar carols play
> And wild and sweet the words repeat of peace on
>   earth, good-will to men!

Through the church bells, God reminded Longfellow of the true peace the baby in the manger brings. As his poem says, "God is not dead, nor doth he sleep." He hasn't abandoned us. The Prince of Peace still triumphs, even in the midst of war and personal tragedy, bringing the peace that passes understanding—peace with God.

Face it. If Jesus came to rid the world of war and suffering, he did a pretty poor job. But what if he brought something greater? What if he did more than anyone ever dared imagine? What if he delivered a unique kind of peace, a peace so great it transcends circumstances? This peace inspired Longfellow to compose this cherished Christmas poem. Jesus promised, "My peace I give you. I do not give to you as the world gives" (John 14:27).

As in Longfellow's day, our generation abounds with trouble and turmoil. And like the great poet, we have a choice: cave in to despair or embrace the peace Jesus offers. Longfellow "heard the bells on Christmas day." His heart was filled with peace, and his life was changed forever.

Principle

Jesus brings a unique peace to mankind that transcends our external circumstances.

Ponder

- What situation in our world and in your life disturbs you most and steals your peace?
- What symbol, like the Christmas bells, might God use to give you a different perspective of your circumstances?

Pursue: For a deeper dive, study Isaiah 9:1–7.

Lord Jesus, thank you for the peace you bring into the world today. Help me embrace your peace that transcends understanding.

The Story

You know the story well. A father makes the ultimate sacrifice and sends his only son to earth to save the race. He enters our world as a tiny baby in a barn and is raised by two commoners in an obscure village. Because of his supernatural power and commitment to truth and justice, he is misunderstood and meets with violent opposition. Eventually at the age of thirty-three, he saves all mankind and renders the forces of evil powerless. He continues to live as our savior. Like I said, you know the story, and this story is, of course, the story of . . . Superman, from the movie *Man of Steel*.

More than coincidence, these parallels between Jesus and Superman speak to something much deeper—our longing for the supernatural. Think of the popularity of every Marvel and DC movie. Hollywood can't crank them out fast enough. And it's not just comic book films—virtually every popular movie contains an element of the supernatural. We have a longing for something beyond our world, placed in our hearts by God himself (Ecclesiastes 3:11).

Many of the stories we love are dim reflections of God's story . . . *The* Story—the story of God's love for us. Unwittingly, Hollywood expresses the truth God places within each heart. We all possess an innate knowledge of God (Romans 1:19), an instinctive sense of right and wrong (Romans 2:14–16), and an awareness that things aren't right in our world (Romans 8:23). Films like *Man of Steel* are humankind's efforts to come to grips with these inner truths. This isn't a bad thing.

Perhaps more than any other time in history, heaven met earth at the incarnation. From start to finish, Christ's birth was immersed in the supernatural. An angel appears to Zechariah. He's literally tongue-tied for nine months, then his lips are supernaturally loosened. Angels appear to Mary, Joseph, the shepherds, and the Magi. A virgin gives birth to the Son of God. Then Elizabeth, Mary, Zechariah, Simeon, and Anna all speak prophetically about the Messiah's birth. How much more supernatural can we get? This is one reason we love Advent. It's saturated in the supernatural.

Superhero stories can be gripping and inspiring. If they speak to you, enjoy them. But they pale in comparison to the Christmas story. This is because the nativity is God's story. The original superhero story. *The Story.*

Principle

So many stories we love are imitations of the story of God's love for us.

Ponder

- In what ways do you sense a longing for the supernatural in your heart?
- How do you express and experience these longings: through being in nature, God's Word, prayer, worship, family, and friends, doing something you love?

Pursue: For a deeper dive, study Romans 5:6–11.

Almighty God, open my heart to you in new ways.
Help me experience your supernatural presence.

Christmas Lights on Valentine's Day

Sara Pascucci received an anonymous letter on February 3. "Take your Christmas lights down! It's Valentine's Day!!!!!!" Even under everyday circumstances this criticism would cause her stress, but that year the demand was "a major blow to the heart," she said.

As was his tradition, her father had put up the decorations after Thanksgiving. And then the unthinkable happened. In mid-January, within one week of each other, both Sara's dad and aunt passed away. Sara was overwhelmed with grief and the busy work that inevitably follows a death.

Sara posted the anonymous letter in a Facebook group, adding her own note. "The family has been preoccupied with funeral arrangements, . . . and just the grieving process of it all. So yes, we haven't gotten around to taking down his Christmas decorations. Be kind to people, because you never know what they are going through."

Sara's neighbors saw her post and almost immediately began sending cards, flowers, meals, and even money to help the family.

Here's the kicker. Neighbors dug out their stored Christmas decorations and put them back up in a compassionate show of solidarity. Just in time for Valentine's Day, Sara's neighborhood glowed with Christmas displays, not only lighting the streets, but lighting her heart as well.[31]

What a great display of the goodwill we should demonstrate at Christmas (or in this case, Valentine's Day). Knowing someone's hurting, we come alongside them in support. Colossians 3:12 tells us, "As God's chosen people, holy and dearly loved, clothe yourselves with compassion, kindness, humility, gentleness and patience." Don't these qualities represent the Savior we worship at Christmas?

Grinches, like the letter-sender, lurk all around us. I've been known to lapse into Grinch-hood on occasion, myself. But in the end, Sara's neighbors, like the Whos of Whoville in the classic Christmas story, win the day. I wouldn't be surprised if the Grinch in this story ended up dragging out her Christmas decorations and displaying them alongside her neighbors.

In the spirit of Sara Pascucci's neighbors, "Merry Christmas!" (Or should I say, "Happy Valentine's Day"?)

Principle

We need to clothe ourselves with kindness, compassion, and humility.

Ponder

- What attribute of Sara Pascucci's neighbors do you appreciate most? How can you model that?
- Who do you know that needs a little extra love and support this Christmas?

Pursue: For a deeper dive, study Colossians 3:5–17.

Lord Jesus, fill me with your kindness, compassion, and humility. Help me to respond with these qualities to others.

Small Beginnings

On March 27, 1964, Alaska experienced the worst earthquake in North American history. The governor appeared on national television to ask American citizens for help. Prior to this plea, he had received a postcard from a boy with two nickels attached. The note read, "Use this wherever it is needed. If you need more, let me know."[32]

It's cute. But it wasn't helpful. Trying to fix Alaska's problem with two nickels would be like trying to fill the Grand Canyon with a handful of dirt. But those two nickels represented something significant: hope. It showed Alaskan citizens that somebody out there cared.

God loves to work with small beginnings.

A manger and a stable—like two nickels compared to the needs of humanity. But from that tiny beginning, the greatest movement in history began—a movement of hope, love, and eternal salvation. Two thousand years later, we look back and rejoice in the birth of our Savior. Titus 2:11 states, "For the grace of God has appeared that offers salvation to all people." The grace of God appeared in that manger, like two nickels on a postcard, and the world was changed forever.

God loves to work with small beginnings.

When the Jews returned to their homeland after a seventy-year exile in Babylon, their first task was to rebuild the temple. But twenty years later, only the foundation stood. God commissioned Zechariah to stir the people to resume building—an overwhelming task the prophet referred to as leveling a mountain. But then he added, "Who dares to despise the day of small things?" (Zechariah 4:10).

God loves to work with small beginnings.

Our lives are filled with a multitude of tasks, especially during the holidays. Perhaps we question the small things we do—housework, paperwork, or people work. But these small beginnings can be just as important—just as holy—as preaching to millions.

God loves to work with small beginnings.

"Who dares to despise the day of small things?" Out of the governor's appeal from two nickels, millions of dollars in donations poured in. Out of a prophet came a temple. And out of a baby in a manger came salvation for humankind. What about the mundane events in your daily life? Well, God loves to work with small beginnings.

Principle

Small beginnings can lead to monumental endings.

Ponder

- When or where have small things made a huge difference in your life?
- What are some of the small things you can do this Christmas season to bring glory to God?

Pursue: For a deeper dive, study Zechariah 4:1–10.

Lord, thank you for small beginnings. In your hands, they can accomplish great things.

The Real Saint Nicholas

Saint Nicholas doesn't live at the North Pole or drive a sleigh pulled by flying reindeer, but he is a source of delight to millions of children who await his magical arrival every Christmas Eve. Who is he—really?

The real-life Saint Nick was Nicholas of Myra, born around AD 280 in modern-day central Turkey. His parents died in his youth, and he gave away his inheritance, taking the words of Jesus literally to "sell everything you have and give to the poor" (Mark 10:21). While still young, he was appointed Bishop of Myra. Because of his faith, Nicholas was imprisoned, tortured, and released. He died on December 6, AD 343.

Many legends surround his life. One tells of a poor neighbor unable to provide a dowry for his daughters. With no dowry, the girls couldn't marry and were destined to be sold into slavery. On three successive nights, Nicholas tossed a bag of gold through the window of their home, which landed in stockings hung by the fire to dry. Thus began the practice of kids hanging stockings on Christmas Eve.

It's also reported that he saved the lives of three innocent men condemned to be executed. Learning of their pending plight, he rushed to the spot of their execution as the sword was about to descend. He snatched it from the executioner's hand and threw it to the ground. The executioner begged his forgiveness, and the prisoners were released.

Several legends center on Saint Nick's protection of children, including one that occurred after his death, where his spirit swooped down to rescue a kidnapped boy and return him to his parents. Another describes Nicholas saving three children who were lost and abducted by an evil butcher. No wonder he's been adored by children through the years.

After sixteen centuries, the line between truth and legend is blurred. But fact or fiction, the stories are fun to tell. Even greater, Saint Nicholas is a symbol of generosity, love, courage, and concern for children. We all need to celebrate these virtues, especially at Christmas, and I need to slow down and appreciate those around me. I need to be generous to those who are marginalized or victimized. I need to defend the innocent. What better symbol of Christmas could we choose than Saint Nicholas, Bishop of Myra, whom Americans know as Santa Claus? He's so much more than a legend. He's a life worth emulating.

Principle

Saint Nicholas provides us with a timeless symbol of the generosity and love Christmas represents.

Ponder

- How does the story of Saint Nicholas inspire you?
- When have you experienced the unselfish generosity exemplified by Nicholas?

Pursue: For a deeper dive, study Mark 10:17–22.

Dear Lord, I'm so thankful for your servants through the years who have modeled humility, generosity, and unconditional love to others. Like Nicholas, help me live out your values.

A Christmas Accident

The Christmas Eve service was scheduled to begin in a few hours at Saint Nicholas Church in Oberndorf, Austria. But the organ was broken, which ruled out performing traditional Christmas carols. Running out of time, Curate Joseph Mohr sat with quill in hand to compose a new song.

Whispering a prayer, Mohr's mind drifted to a family with a newborn child he'd recently visited. He recalled the mother holding the infant wrapped snugly against her, and words flowed onto the paper. A simple refrain emerged, as if heaven itself was penning the words. Franz Gruber, a local schoolmaster, created a tune to complement Mohr's lyrics.

That evening Mohr played the guitar and sang tenor while Gruber sang bass. The choir joined in four-part harmony on each refrain. The last-minute, wasn't-supposed-to-happen song, "Silent Night," stirred every listener's heart.

This is almost where the story ended. A few years passed, and once again the faltering organ needed repair. The organ-tuner discovered the sheet music, and with Gruber's consent, obtained a copy. He played the song wherever he traveled, and its popularity spread throughout Europe, then to America, and ultimately worldwide.[33]

"Silent Night" remains the quintessential Christmas carol. It adds an element of wonder to Christmas Eve services as lights are dimmed, candles lit, and members softly sing. Translated into over three hundred languages, it is designated an item of Intangible Cultural Heritage by UNESCO.

"Silent Night" has powerfully impacted innumerable lives. Just playing it has been known to break up bar fights. Like me, many are unable to hold back tears when they pause and absorb the simple lyrics and tune of this carol.

But it almost didn't happen. I'm convinced God guided Mohr and Gruber that Christmas Eve in 1818. A string of events fell into place, enabling us to experience this cherished, life-changing hymn—just as the events in Bethlehem fell into place two thousand years ago. A deluge of difficulties could have prevented Christ's birth from occurring at any point, but God was present, guiding the process.

Philippians 2:13 states that God is working in our lives "in order to fulfill his good purpose." If misfortunes occur this Christmas, as they did for Joseph Mohr, relax. They may lead to a life-transforming event, remembered by many for decades to come.

Principle

When misfortunes occur, God is in the process, guiding us to transform other lives.

Ponder

- Like Joseph Mohr, when have you experienced a so-called accident that God's hand was guiding?
- How can you keep your spiritual eyes attuned to misfortunes that God might turn into blessings this Christmas season?

Pursue: For a deeper dive, study Philippians 2:12–18.

God, you are great, and you are good. Only you can take the misfortunes in our lives and turn them into blessings.

Performing on God's Stage

The young girl's hands trembled as she faced the crowd. Singing a solo before three hundred people at a Christmas Eve service would produce fear in the most stalwart vocalist. As she sang, her six-year-old voice rang out with surprising confidence. As I stood onstage, something caught my eye, and I teared up. A woman, obviously the girl's mother, knelt in front of her daughter, smiling and mouthing the words for her to follow. The girl stared intently at her mom, as if singing to an audience of one. As her daughter struggled with nervousness, the mother communicated an unspoken message of unconditional encouragement.

Likewise, as we perform on life's stage, circumstances can seem downright overwhelming. Distractions and challenges can weigh us down. Rather than fixating on the audience of three hundred around us, what if we focused on the audience of One? Psalm 123:2 tells us, "As the eyes of slaves look to the hand of their master, as the eyes of a female slave look to the hand of her mistress, so our eyes look to the LORD our God, till he shows us his mercy."

Shouldn't Christmas be the easiest time of year to stay focused on Jesus? Everywhere we look we see reminders of the birth of our Lord. But if you're like me, you're far too distracted by holiday hassles. When you discover you're overdrawn at the bank and only halfway done with your shopping list, unholy thoughts and unsanctified words easily rise to the surface.

When holiday humbug sucks the joy out of our celebration, we need to take a deep breath and fix our eyes on the One who can restore our peace. Focusing on our circumstances leads to fear and anxiety. Centering on Jesus brings peace and confidence. "Fixing our eyes on Jesus" is the solution offered in Hebrews 12:2. Doesn't this sound so much better than popping Tums every hour because we're so stressed?

Settle into an easy chair with a hot cup of cocoa in hand and Christmas music in the background. Turn your eyes on Jesus—even for a few minutes. As you do, you'll discover a profound truth: God is for you. He's always with you, rooting for you and mouthing the words to the song he has put in your heart—for an audience of one.

Principle

Keep your eyes fixed on Jesus this holiday season.

Ponder

- What distractions pull you away from focusing on Jesus?
- What calms your heart and helps you shift your attention away from your problems and toward Jesus?

Pursue: For a deeper dive, study Psalm 123.

Heavenly Father, in the hectic holiday rush, help me stay focused on you. When I get distracted, turn my attention away from the mess so I can see you.

It's a Wonderful Life

After viewing the film a quadrillion times, you'd think I'd grow weary of it, but I'm compelled to watch this classic each holiday season—*Pippi Longstocking's Christmas*. No . . . absolutely not. I'm speaking of *It's a Wonderful Life*. I think watching the movie should be a requirement for US citizenship. Well, that may be a bit extreme . . . maybe.

In the film, Jimmy Stewart plays George Bailey, a man who sacrifices his dreams to stay in his hometown of Bedford Falls. On Christmas Eve, the family building and loan company experiences a financial crisis, and George faces almost-certain imprisonment. In the depths of despair, he considers suicide but is saved by his guardian angel, Clarence. Clarence gives George a rare gift: the ability to see what the world would be like if he had never been born.

The results are disastrous. His friends are losers, and his town is corrupt. Clarence shows George how important each of us are. He states, "Strange, isn't it? Each man's life touches so many other lives. When he isn't around, he leaves an awful hole, doesn't he?"[34] In the end, his friends rally and pay the $8,000 needed to preserve the building and loan company and keep George out of jail.

Like a pebble cast into a pond causes ripples that reach the other side, small acts done in Jesus's name can go far beyond their source. We influence someone, who influences someone, who influences someone, who . . . you get the picture. Minute actions cause a chain reaction of events, sometimes producing gigantic results.

Isn't this the message of the manger? A small, seemingly insignificant baby transformed the world. Jesus said, "If you give even a cup of cold water to one of the least of my followers, you will surely be rewarded" (Matthew 10:42 NLT). A cup of cold water—another small offering. How could this make a difference? Let God figure it out.

What more significant message could we carry through Christmas and into the new year? You don't need to be an eloquent preacher or sing like an angel. If God calls you to serve him in mundane ways, whether it's working in a building and loan company or caring for kids, you can trust him to handle the rest. Helen Keller said, "It is my chief duty and joy to accomplish humble tasks as though they were great and noble."[35]

Don't wait for your guardian angel to show you what life would be like if you'd never been born. As George Bailey learned, stay faithful to do the seemingly insignificant tasks and relish the wonderful life God has given you.

Principle

Serve God in the mundane things and trust him to handle the rest.

Ponder

- In what mundane matters can you serve God during this holiday season?
- What goals can you set in the coming year to help you appreciate the wonderful life God has given you?

Pursue: For a deeper dive, study Matthew 10:40–42.

Lord, deliver me from thinking I have to do something considered great. Help me to serve others, then trust you with the results.

The Answer Is Jesus

As the Christmas Eve service began, the pastor invited all the kids to the front for a short children's message. He began by describing an animal with antlers and a bushy tail. "Can you guess what I'm describing?" No response. "It's brown and is very popular this time of year. There's even a song about it." He paused, certain that one of the tykes would guess the answer. Silence. He couldn't believe it, so out of desperation he said, "It pulls a sleigh and has a red blinking nose."

Finally, one little boy timidly raised his hand and replied, "I know the answer is supposed to be Jesus, but it sure sounds like Rudolph the red-nosed reindeer to me!"[36]

This young lad inadvertently uncovered a struggle many of us face. He wanted to give the correct religious answer, but no matter how hard he tried, it just didn't work. How true this is of many of our pat answers to the challenging questions of life. Too often we lock ourselves into our own religious boxes and miss the obvious.

But here's something even more profound. In a sense, Jesus *is* the answer. He's the answer to all the deep, meaningful questions that trouble our lives. Jesus is the answer to the loneliness that plagues millions during the holiday season (Matthew 28:20). Jesus is the answer to the hopelessness that gnaws at the souls of those who feel like giving up (1 Peter 1:3). Jesus is the answer to the spiritual darkness that engulfs our world and results in violence, human trafficking, and abortion (John 8:12). Jesus is the answer to the instability and lack of purpose that characterize our times (Matthew 7:24–27).

Jesus is the Alpha and Omega—the beginning and the end—everything from A to Z. He's our Living Hope, the Light of the

World, and our Rock. He's the sum of all that is beautiful, righteous, and true.

Whatever question plagues you; whatever struggles you face—whether during the Christmas season or throughout the year—we can say with confidence, Jesus is the answer.

Principle

Jesus is the answer to all that matters.

Ponder

- In what ways have you found Jesus to be the answer to all your needs?
- In what areas of your life do you need to seek the answers Jesus offers?

Pursue: For a deeper dive, study Revelation 1:10–20.

Lord Jesus, there are so many unfulfilled needs in my life. Please saturate me with your presence and help me know you really are the answer to all my needs.

I've Got a Secret

It was a glorious Christmas moment. We couldn't have planned it better. My son Josh was eight years old. For months, he had expressed his desire for a BB gun for Christmas. Much like Ralphie in the film *A Christmas Story*, he spoke of little else. We purchased the weapon, despite our well-warranted fears that he might "shoot his eye out," and snuck it into my in-laws' home.

Christmas morning arrived. When the chaos of opening presents ceased, and we wearily sat on the couch, I mimicked the routine from *A Christmas Story*. "Did you get everything you wanted, Josh?"

He shrugged. "I guess so," sounding as gloomy as a mortician.

The relatives concentrated on Josh, not wanting to miss his reaction to what would happen next. "Say, what's that behind the tree?" I asked.

Josh turned and saw the box. He leapt toward it like a gazelle, grabbed it, and opened it in world-record time. "No way!" he exclaimed, holding it aloft. Everyone cheered. We had pulled it off—a genuine Christmas secret. The clandestine nature of the event brought much more joy than merely handing him a box to open. Our mystery would have put a smile on Agatha Christie's face.

So much of Christ's birth was shrouded in secrecy—a mystery. Most were clueless about what God was up to, but God revealed his secret to Zechariah, Mary, Joseph, the shepherds, and the Magi.

Think about Joseph. God spoke to him in a dream, telling him to take the baby and flee to Egypt. Then, as in an espionage thriller, the trio stole away in the night, escaping from Bethlehem before Herod carried out his plan to murder innocent children.

Likewise, much of the Christmas message lands on each of us

secretly. We hear God's voice speaking to us through Scripture, music, or simply a sense of peace during this season. The third verse of "O Little Town of Bethlehem" echoes this thought.

> How silently, how silently the wondrous gift is giv'n
> So God imparts to human hearts the blessings of his
> heav'n
> No ear may hear his coming, but in this world of sin,
> Where meek souls will receive him still, the dear
> Christ enters in.

The greatest gift we could receive this Christmas is for our dear Christ to enter our hearts, as he loves to do, secretly and silently.

Principle
God often operates in secrecy, working behind the scenes to accomplish his purposes.

Ponder
- When have you encountered God in a secret way?
- Of all the secrets in the nativity story, which is the most meaningful to you?

Pursue: For a deeper dive, study Colossians 1:24–2:3.

> *Lord, thank you for making known to me the mystery you planned before the creation of the world, which is Christ in me. There is no greater blessing I could receive this Christmas.*

An Ordinary Night

An ordinary night. Stars twinkled like a blanket of diamonds stretched across the sky. Sheep slept peacefully under the eye of their shepherds. An evening breeze chilled the air. An ordinary night . . . but then the extraordinary broke through.

A blinding flash split the sky. A magnificent heavenly being hovered overhead. All the shepherds fell to the ground, trembling in terror. But the angel spoke words of comfort. "Do not be afraid. I bring you good news that will cause great joy for all the people. Today in the town of David a Savior has been born to you; he is the Messiah, the Lord. This will be a sign to you: You will find a baby wrapped in cloths and lying in a manger" (Luke 2:10–12).

Instantly, thousands of radiant beings crowded the sky, singing, "Glory to God in the highest heaven, and on earth peace to those on whom his favor rests" (Luke 2:14). Then the angels vanished. Rising slowly, no one spoke. Finally, a shepherd declared, "The Messiah has been born! Let's hurry to Bethlehem and see him with our own eyes!" Down the hills they descended, pondering why the angel had said the Messiah would be lying in a feeding trough. They found him, possibly in a limestone cave that had been converted into a stable.

There he slept. A few hours old, yet existing from all eternity. Powerless, yet all-powerful. Unable to speak, yet his words had birthed the stars. The great I Am encased in flesh. The shepherds fell to their knees in worship.

Eventually they returned to their flocks, but their lives were never the same. The shepherds had encountered Almighty God face-to-face.

For thousands of years, humanity had cowered beneath the bondage of sin and death—but now they were free. The Savior was born!

Amazing that God chose lowly shepherds to be his Son's first visitors—not the governor or high priest. This is *not* how we would have done it—but it's one of numerous paradoxes surrounding the incarnation. I suppose the Lord wanted us to know that he came for all men, not only for the wealthy and powerful but also for each of us— the common, the helpless, and the unknown.

And he still comes. Today, let's open our hearts and worship him as the shepherds did. Like them, our lives will never be the same.

Principle

The night of Christ's birth was an ordinary night, but also a night like no other.

Ponder

- What aspects of that extraordinary night touch you the most?
- How might you encounter Jesus in a powerful way as the shepherds did?

Pursue: For a deeper dive, study Luke 2:8–20.

Lord Jesus, I worship you this day, just as the shepherds did, as my King and Savior who delivers me from death and restores life to my soul.

'Twas the Day *After* Christmas

It's over. Christmas has come and gone. The shopping, the cheesy TV shows and performances, the trip to Grandma's. Candy canes, turkey and gravy, giving and receiving gifts. Another celebration is behind us. But there's a sense in which Christmas isn't over at all. It's only begun.

Christmas began with a baby—God himself—entering our world. But this was just the start. He grew into a man, left his carpentry shop, and ventured out into our world with a message—a whole new way of life he called the kingdom of heaven. He came to bring heaven to earth. It's the life God desired for each of us before he created the universe. He inserted himself into our world so we could live in his, so we could experience his best for us. God always wants more for us than we want for ourselves.

For many of us, the day after Christmas is second only to April 15 as the most difficult day of the year. It's a letdown after the Christmas crescendo. The Advent season is a time when the world in some small way is what it ought to be. Elvis Presley captured this sense in his song "Why Can't Every Day Be Like Christmas?" It represents that wordless longing for God to set things right in our world because we sense that life is not what it ought to be. Deep inside, this is why we love Christmas. It reminds us of how God *has* set things right. At Christmas, we experience a small taste of heaven.

So let's pause before we return to the rat race. As we wave goodbye to another December 25, how can we hold on to Christmas a little longer?

We can start by carrying Christ's spirit of service into everyday life. We can bring heaven to earth for the rest of the year. When a driver cuts us off, we can smile and wave. When we encounter a homeless person, we can make eye contact and greet them. We can help an elderly neighbor put out her garbage, even if she's cranky. We can take time to listen to our family members and show them we *really* care.

Simple acts of kindness have the power to change others' lives. We can display the spirit of Christmas 365 days a year. Like the babe in the manger, let's change our world, a little bit every day, starting right now, on the day after Christmas.

Principle

We can display the spirit of Christmas 365 days a year.

Ponder

- How has your life been changed this Christmas season?
- What commitments can you make to live out the spirit of Christmas in the year ahead?

Pursue: For a deeper dive, study Luke 15.

Jesus, thank you for coming into our world. But even more, thank you for the new life you bring to each of us. Help me to live in the spirit of Christmas every day.

A Life-Changing Decision

John 3:16 states, "For God so loved the world that he gave his one and only Son, that whoever believes in him shall not perish but have eternal life."

I pray these devotions have blessed you and that you have been reassured or have come to believe that Jesus truly is who he claimed to be, God in human form. If you believe Jesus died for your sins and was raised from the dead, then your next step is to declare your faith in him.

Romans 10:9–10 says, "If you declare with your mouth, 'Jesus is Lord,' and believe in your heart that God raised him from the dead, you will be saved. For it is with your heart that you believe and are justified [restored to a right relationship with God], and it is with your mouth that you profess your faith and are saved." Ask Jesus to forgive you and save you from your sins.

Then find a church that honors the Bible as God's Word and be baptized (immersed) in water, which is a public declaration of faith in the death, burial, and resurrection of Jesus (Romans 6:3–6). Your commitment will set you on a new path in life as a follower of Jesus. You can begin to experience eternal life right now and know the love, joy, and peace the babe in the manger brought into our world.

Notes

1. Based on a message by Jeff Walling, "The Messy Messiah Who Joined Our Mess," Church Leaders, April 8, 2014, https://churchleaders.com/pastors/videos-for-pastors/173835 -the-messy-messiah-who-joined-our-mess.html.

2. Yann Martel, *Life of Pi* (Edinburgh, Scotland: Canongate Books, 2012), 61.

3. "Baby's Birth Saves Family from Tornado," CNN, accessed March 18, 2022, https://www.cnn.com/videos/us/2012 /03/07/dnt-wlwt-ky-baby-saves-family-tornado.wlwt.

4. Trevin Wax, "We Lepers—An Unusual Christmas Meditation," The Gospel Coalition, December 22, 2011, https://www.thegospelcoalition.org/blogs/trevin-wax /we-lepers-an-unusual-christmas-meditation-2/.

5. "Rebellious Innkeeper," *The Pastor's Story File*, 15, no. 2 (December 1998).

6. "The Three Wiseguys," Sermon Central, January 14, 2003, https://www.sermoncentral.com/sermon-illustrations/11672 /the-three-wiseguys-by-sermon-central.

7. "The 2021 Neiman Marcus Fantasy Gifts," Neiman Marcus, accessed September 15, 2022, https://www.neimanmarcus.com /editorial/gift-guides-holiday-and-special-events/fantasy-gifts.

8. Sandro Contenta, "The Shepherds: The Bible's 'Biker Gang,'" *Toronto Star*, December 20, 2009, https://www.thestar.com /life/2009/12/20/the_shepherds_the_bibles_biker_gang.html.

9. John Welch, "The Significance of Bethlehem," Countryside Community Church, accessed March 16, 2022, https://countrysidechurchoro.ca/the-significance-of-bethlehem/.

10. Donald Miller, *Blue Like Jazz: Nonreligious Thoughts on Christian Spirituality* (Nashville: Thomas Nelson, 2003), 33–34.

11. Daniel Im, "The (Hidden) Theology and History of O Come O Come Emmanuel," DanielIm.com, December 19, 2017, https://www.danielim.com/2017/12/19/the-hidden-theology-and-history-of-o-come-o-come-emmanuel/.

12. Bruce Marshall, *The World, the Flesh and Father Smith* (New York: Houghton Mifflin Company, 1945), 108.

13. Max Lucado, *The Applause of Heaven* (Nashville: Word Publishing Group, 1996), 73.

14. Christopher J Wiles, "Wise Men and a Kingdom Turned Upside Down," *Seriously? The Goal-Oriented Christian Life* (blog), December 22, 2016, https://devotionalstsf.org/2016/12/22/wise-men-and-a-kingdom-turned-upside-down-matthew-21-12/.

15. "Rudolph the Red-Nosed Reindeer," Wikipedia, accessed March 16, 2022, https://en.wikipedia.org/wiki/Rudolph_the_Red-Nosed_Reindeer.

16. Liam Barnes, "Author of Christmas Letter to Santa Found by Chimney Sweeps Revealed," BBC News, July 29, 2021, https://www.bbc.com/news/uk-england-nottinghamshire-58006173.

17. Eugene "Red" McDaniel, *Scars and Stripes: The True Story of One Man's Courage Facing Death as a POW in Vietnam* (Chicago: WND Books, 2012), 145.

18. Gene Edwards, *The Birth* (Jacksonville, FL: SeedSowers Publishing, 1990), 88–89.

19. "White Elephant Gift Exchange," Wikipedia, accessed March 18, 2022, https://en.wikipedia.org/wiki/White_elephant_gift_exchange.

20. Adapted from a sermon by Rick Warren, "Christmas Eve 1992: What Difference Does Christmas Make?," December 24, 1992, https://store.pastors.com/1992-non-series-sermons.html.

21. "*Messiah* (Handel)," Wikipedia, accessed April 25, 2024, https://en.wikipedia.org/wiki/Messiah_(Handel).

22. Joseph E. McCabe, *Handel's Messiah: A Devotional Commentary* (Philadelphia: Westminster Press, 1978), 27.

23. Max Lucado, *In the Eye of the Storm* (Nashville: Word Publishing, 1991), 48–49.

24. Desiree Kocis, "Did a Grumman F11 Tiger Shoot Itself Down?," *Plane and Pilot*, October 4, 2021, https://www.planeandpilotmag.com/news/pilot-talk/grumman-f11-tiger-shoot-itself-down/.

25. Michael Stark, "The King and the Maiden: Kierkegaard's Christmas Parable," Former Aspiring Philosopher, December 14, 2015, https://formeraspiringphilosopher.com/2015/12/14/the-king-the-maiden-kierkegaards-christmas-parable/.

26. H. T. Webster, "Hardin County, 1809," Press Publishing Company, 1918, reprinted in Merrill D. Peterson, *Lincoln in American Memory* (New York: Oxford University Press, 1994), 181.

27. "Herod the Great: A Life of Intrigue, Architecture, and Cruelty," Church of the Great God, September 12, 2008, https://www.cgg.org/index.cfm/library/article/id/1387/herod-great.htm.

28. Heartland News, "Christmas Card Takes 93 Years to Reach Destination," KFVS12, December 18, 2007, https://www.kfvs12.com/story/7513207/christmas-card-takes-93-years-to-reach-destination/.

29. C. S. Lewis, *Mere Christianity* (New York: MacMillan, 1952), 51.

30. Erin Zimmerman, "The Story behind the Song: I Heard the Bells on Christmas Day," CBN, December 10, 2022, https://www1.cbn.com/story-behind-song-i-heard-bells-christmas-day.

31. "She Was Shamed for Still Having Christmas Lights Up," Preaching Today, accessed September 1, 2022, https://www.preachingtoday.com/illustrations/2021/march/she-was-shamed-for-still-having-christmas-lights-up.html.

32. "Is the World Ready for Christmas?," *The Pastor's Story File*, 15, no. 2 (December 1998).

33. "Glorious Gift from Christmas Past," *Reader's Digest*, December 1993, 69–72.

34. *It's a Wonderful Life*, directed by Frank Capra (California: Liberty Films, 1946).

35. Helen Keller, *Optimism: An Essay* (New York: T. Y. Crowell and Company, 1903), 21.

36. Jon Good, "It Sounds like Rudolph the Red-Nosed Reindeer," SermonNews, December 2009. Emailed to the author. Used by permission.

About the Author

Barney Cargile and his wife, Linda, were married fifty years before she passed from this life into eternity. Cargile lives on their small organic farm in Santa Rosa, California. He serves as community pastor with Santa Rosa Christian Church and works with The Ark, a sober living house, and the Redwood Gospel Mission. His greatest joys are traveling, teaching, and playing "monster" with his grandkids.

He bases his life on Jesus's statement: "If you remain in me and I in you, you will bear much fruit" (John 15:5). He is passionate about partnering with God to free those in spiritual and psychological bondage. He has traveled extensively, training pastors in a dozen nations. He publishes a weekly devotional blog, *Barney's Bullet*.

For information on Barney's future books or to subscribe to his weekly blog, please visit BarneyCargile.com or email him at barneyc3@gmail.com.

Spread the Word
by Doing One Thing.

- Give a copy of this book as a gift.

- Share the QR code link via your social media.

- Write a review of this book on your blog, favorite bookseller's website, or at ODB.org/store.

- Recommend this book to your church, small group, or book club.

Connect with us. ⓕ ⓘ

Our Daily Bread Publishing
PO Box 3566, Grand Rapids, MI 49501, USA
Email: books@odb.org

Love God. Love Others.

with  Our Daily Bread.

Your gift changes lives.

Connect with us. [f] [○]

Our Daily Bread Publishing
PO Box 3566, Grand Rapids, MI 49501, USA
Email: books@odb.org